The First Book of

UNIX®

The First Book of

UNIX®

Douglas Topham

SAMS

A Division of Macmillan Computer Publishing

11711 North College, Carmel, Indiana 46032 USA

FIRST EDITION
FOURTH PRINTING—1991

International Standard Book Number: 0-672-27299-7
Library of Congress Catalog Card Number: 89-63708

Acquisitions Editor: *Scott Arant*
Development Editor: *C. Herbert Feltner and Marie Butler-Knight*
Manuscript Editor: *Gary Masters*
Production Coordinator: *Katherine Stuart Ewing*
Illustrator: *Don Clemons*
Cover Artist: *Held & Diedrich Design*
Indexer: *Hilary Adams*
Technical Reviewer: *Russell Sage*
Compositor: *Joe Ramon*

Printed in the United States of America

Trademark Acknowledgments

Contents

Preface, ix

Conventions Used in This Book, xi

1 Introduction to UNIX, 1

What You Will Learn, 1
What is an Operating System?, 1
How Does UNIX Differ from DOS?, 3
Some Typical Configurations, 6
UNIX and Standards, 8
Getting Started, 11
What You've Learned, 18
Chapter 1 Quiz, 19

2 The File System, 21

What You Will Learn, 21
An Overview of the File System, 22
Handling Directories, 25
Handling Files, 28
File Permissions, 36
What You've Learned, 40
Chapter 2 Quiz, 40

3 *Processing Commands, 43*

What You Will Learn, *43*
The Different Shell Programs, *43*
Commands and Command Lines, *44*
Redirection of Input and Output, *47*
Connecting Processes, *51*
Background Processing, *53*
Executing Commands from Files, *56*
The Initialization Files, *61*
What You've Learned, *65*
Chapter 3 Quiz, *66*

4 *Some Utility Programs, 69*

What You Will Learn, *69*
Displaying a Calendar, *69*
Displaying Text on the Screen, *71*
Printing, *73*
Finding Files, *78*
Searching for Text in a File, *82*
Sorting Lines in a File, *86*
Performing Calculations, *90*
What You've Learned, *93*
Chapter 4 Quiz, *93*

5 *Editing with vi, 95*

What You Will Learn, *95*
Beginning and Ending an Editing Session, *95*
Moving the Cursor and the Screen Display, *98*
Adjusting the Screen Display, *104*
Entering New Text, *107*
Deleting Text, *112*
Moving Text, *116*
Finding and Replacing Text, *119*
What You've Learned, *121*
Chapter 5 Quiz, *124*

6 *Communicating with Other Users,* 127

What You Will Learn, *127*
Internal Communication, *127*
External Communication, *136*
Using the UNIX Bulletin Board, *145*
What You've Learned, *150*
Chapter 6 Quiz, *151*

7 *Formatting Text,* 153

What You Will Learn, *153*
Formatting UNIX Documents, *153*
Formatting Paragraphs, *156*
Formatting Display Text, *157*
Formatting Lists, *160*
Other Formatting Features, *166*
What You've Learned, *170*
Chapter 7 Quiz, *170*

8 *System Administration,* 173

What You Will Learn, *173*
The System Administrator, *173*
Working with Users, *176*
Backing Up Files, *182*
Setting Up Terminals, *188*
Self-Running Processes, *194*
Another Look at Permissions, *196*
Shutting the System Down, *199*
What You've Learned, *201*
Chapter 8 Quiz, *202*

A *Glossary,* 205

B *Quick Reference,* 233

vii

C The C Shell, *261*

C Shell Initialization Files, *261*
Retrieving Command Lines, *264*
Selecting Arguments on a Command Line, *266*
Changing a Command Line, *269*
Using Abbreviations, *270*

Answers to Quizzes, *273*

Index, *277*

viii

Preface

This book introduces the features of UNIX that are most useful to a new user. You will learn how to begin working on UNIX System V immediately. However, this book covers only those features suitable for beginners; it contains no programming or highly technical information.

Chapter 1 introduces you to operating systems and UNIX and then shows you how to log in and start working right away. You'll learn about file administration in Chapter 2 and about command processing in Chapter 3. These three chapters provide you with a solid foundation for understanding how to use the UNIX system.

Chapter 4 demonstrates how to use many of the most common utility programs. These utilities let you perform many important tasks that you must use all the time, such as printing, searching, and sorting.

Chapter 5 offers a thorough introduction to text-editing with the built-in vi (visual interpreter) program. You'll learn how to adjust the screen display, insert and delete text, move text, search for text, and replace text. These skills will enable you to create and edit documents with confidence.

Chapter 6 shows you how to communicate with other users on your own UNIX system and on other systems using electronic mail and a UNIX network called uucp. With the skills you learn in this chapter, you will be able to send and receive messages to many other users and use a bulletin board.

Chapter 7 explains how to use the mm program to format text before printing your documents. After reviewing the tools provided by UNIX, you will learn how to format paragraphs, display text, and create lists. You will also learn how to justify text, skip lines, highlight text, and change point size.

Finally, Chapter 8 shows you how to perform several basic administrative tasks. You will learn how to set up new user accounts, determine who is logged in, back up files, set up terminals, work with self-running processes, read numeric permissions, and shut the system down. There is a lot more to learn about system administration, but this chapter will give you a good start.

In each chapter, you will go through a number of simple step-by-step exercises to learn the basic information. A chapter summary and a quiz help to reinforce your understanding of the subject. No knowledge of mathematics or programming is required.

X

Conventions Used in This Book

Filenames and commands are shown in monospace text. For example, in the following example, `cat` represents the name of a command, and `chapter1` is the name of a file:

```
$ cat chapter1
```

Generic names are shown in italic. For example, in the following example, *file* represents any file with any name:

```
$ cat file
```

Major steps in a procedure are numbered; subordinate steps are preceded by triangular bullets, as follows:

1. Request a password change:
    ► Type `passwd` and press Enter (or Return):
    ```
    $ passwd
    Changing password for larry
    Old password: _
    ```
    ► Type your current password and press Enter (or Return).
2. Enter a new password:
    ► Enter your new password:
    ```
    Old password:
    New password:
    Retype your new password: _
    ```

Enter your new password again:
```
Retype your new password:
$ _
```

A list of items from which you may choose is surrounded by brackets, as illustrated here:

-size   [+b]   more than b
                                 blocks

             [b]   exactly b blocks

             [-b]   fewer than b
                                 blocks

xii

Chapter 1

Introduction to UNIX

What You Will Learn

This chapter introduces you to the UNIX operating system. It assumes that you have used a computer and that you have some knowledge of the Disk Operating System (DOS) used on IBM and IBM-compatible PCs. This chapter discusses the following topics:

- ► What is an operating system?
- ► How UNIX differs from DOS.
- ► Some typical UNIX system configurations.
- ► Standard versions of UNIX.
- ► How you log into UNIX and start using the system.

What Is an Operating System?

An operating system is the software that allows a computer's hardware and software to work together. It consists of programs and routines that coordinate processes, translate data from input and output devices, regulate data storage in memory, and allocate tasks to different processors. It also provides programs and functions that help programmers develop new software.

An operating system provides two related functions: a standard programming environment for software developers and a standard working environment for users.

People use computers to perform work with the aid of application programs. An operating system furthers this end by making it easier for programmers to develop these programs and by making it easier for users to run these programs. Thus, an operating system facilitates the use of computers by aiding and standardizing both the creation and use of application programs.

Software Development

An operating system permits programmers to develop software for many types of computers by making different computers act in a similar manner. Without a standardized operating system, a programmer would have to learn all the hardware intricacies and idiosyncrasies of every different computer system. However, an operating system masks differences in hardware and lets the programmer manipulate a variety of computers in the same way.

Because programmers can focus their work on the standard environment provided by the operating system, they can work more efficiently and develop more software in less time. This creates an upward spiral of activity in which the greater availability of programs promotes the use of computers that run the operating system.

Software Usage

Just as an operating system provides a common programming environment for software developers, it also provides a common working environment for users of computers. An operating system provides a standardized method for starting a computing session, storing files, working with files, accessing peripheral devices, and ending a computing session.

The user can concentrate on working rather than on learning how to perform basic tasks on a variety of different computers. Because an operating system provides standard commands and

2

procedures, a user can begin a job on one machine, continue the job on another, and then complete the job on the first machine.

From the point of view of a user, the operating system remains secondary. The application program is always the user's primary concern. However, the operating system is always in the background, supporting the application program in many different ways with many essential services.

How Does UNIX Differ from DOS?

The main difference between UNIX and DOS is that DOS was originally designed for single-user systems, while UNIX was designed for systems with many users. Many other differences between the two systems derive from this fundamental difference.

3

Common Characteristics

UNIX and DOS both provide users with an assortment of commands to be entered for processing. A prompt appears on the screen, the user types a command according to some pre-defined syntax, and then the user presses the Enter (or Return) key to initiate processing. After the task has been completed, the prompt reappears. As we approach the 1990s, both operating systems are beginning to offer graphical interfaces with screen icons and mouse control.

Note, however, that UNIX is a multitasking operating system, which means that a user can run more than one program at a time. A single user could run three or four tasks simultaneously.

DOS was originally patterned after its predecessor for personal computers, CP/M (control program/monitor). Since its introduction late in 1981, however, DOS has been strongly influenced by UNIX. The inclusion of directories and subdirectories and the addition of new commands to support these structures are the most obvious influences of UNIX on the later versions of DOS.

Table 1-1 shows some of the important commands in these two operating systems. Note that several commands perform similar functions. In fact, some commands are identical (or nearly identical) in both operating systems.

Table 1-1. Corresponding Commands

UNIX Command	DOS Command	Function
ls	dir	Display the contents of the current directory
cd	cd	Change directories (move from one directory to another)
mkdir	md	Create a new subdirectory under the current directory
rmdir	rd	Delete (or remove) an existing directory
cat	type	Display the contents of a file
cp	copy	Copy a file (or a group of files)
mv	ren	Rename a file
rm	del	Delete a file (or a group of files)
ln	–	Form a link to a file
chmod	–	Set file permissions
cal	–	Display a calendar for a year or month
lp	print	Queue a file for printing
pstat	print	Display the printing queue
find	–	List filenames that meet criteria
grep	find	List lines in a file that meet criteria
sort	sort	Sort lines in a file
dc	–	Start the desk calculator
bc	–	Start the high-precision calculator
vi	edlin	Create and edit text
write	–	Send a message to another terminal
calendar	–	Send a reminder to yourself
mail	–	Send electronic mail to another user
cu	–	Call another system
uucp	–	Communicate with other system
nroff	–	Format text for printing (fixed width)
troff	–	Format text for printing (variable width)
cpio	xcopy	Back up and recover files

4

Text Processing and Formatting

In UNIX, extensive text-processing and text-formatting features are included with the operating system. UNIX provides `vi` (the visual interpreter) and `nroff` and `troff` (the text formatters for daisy-wheel printers, typesetters, and laser printers). This follows the tradition of mainframe operating systems.

In DOS, text-processing and text-formatting that approach the level of sophistication of `vi` and `nroff` and `troff` can be found only in application programs. DOS provides only a simple and extremely limited line editor called `edlin`.

Programming Tools

UNIX also includes extensive programming tools with the operating system. UNIX provides a built-in programming language for the command processor (also called the *shell*), the C programming language, and a variety of debuggers, analyzers, compilers, and other tools.

DOS provides a debugger, along with BASIC. DOS allows automated operation through batch files, but these are less sophisticated than the programming structures offered in the shell scripts of the UNIX system.

5

System Administration

As a relatively large system with many users, each UNIX site requires a system administrator. The system administrator sets up new accounts for users, assigns passwords, installs terminals and printers, starts and stops the system, backs up files, provides system security, and helps new users. The software tools that aid the system administrator are, naturally, included with UNIX.

As a single-machine operating system, DOS can be maintained and administered much more easily. A user generally is responsible only for less involved tasks, such as initializing the system and backing up files. Tools for performing these tasks are available within DOS, but more elegant and sophisticated programs are often available as separate third-party application programs.

Some Typical Configurations

UNIX generally is not run on a single computer, but on a group of connected machines. This section describes some typical configurations of machines connected for the purpose of running UNIX, including the following:

Terminals and a minicomputer

Stand-alone workstations

Workstations in a local area network

PC-based systems

Terminals and Minicomputer

6

This is the "traditional" configuration, which dates back to the earliest days of the UNIX system. A minicomputer with a large memory and disk capacity, such as a VAX, performs the processing, while users access the host computer using "dumb" terminals. The terminals are connected directly to the minicomputer through a communications device that allows many incoming lines. See Figure 1-1 for a diagram of this configuration.

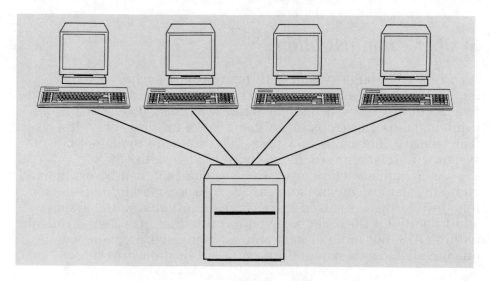

Figure 1-1. Terminals Connected to a Minicomputer

Stand-Alone Workstations

This configuration has become widely used in the 1980s, mainly through the efforts of Sun Microsystems and Apollo Computers. It is similar to the terminal configuration described previously, but each workstation also has its own processing power. A user can work locally on the workstation, but also can switch it online to log into the UNIX system on the minicomputer. Figure 1-2 depicts this configuration.

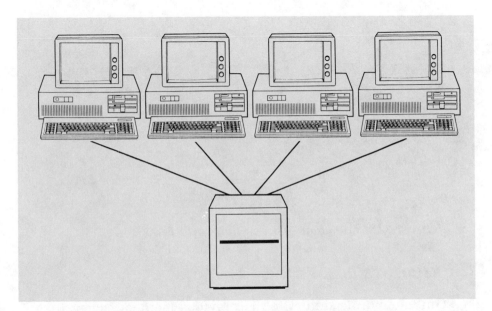

7

Figure 1-2. Stand-Alone Workstations Connected to a Minicomputer

Workstations in a Local Area Network

Another approach is to connect a group of workstations together in a local area network (LAN), using one of the workstations as a *file server*. This is more economical than the previous two configurations. As with stand-alone workstations, users can use DOS locally and then switch to UNIX on the server. An example of this configuration is shown in Figure 1-3.

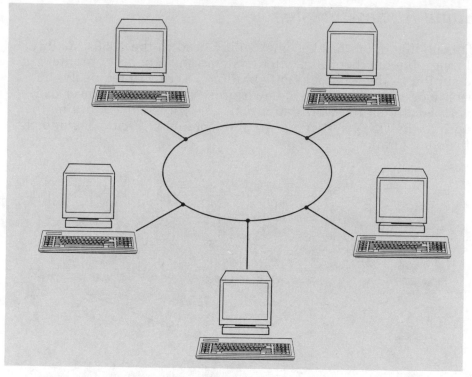

Figure 1-3. Stand-Alone Workstations in a LAN

PC-Based Systems

This configuration is similar to the previous method, except that personal computers are used instead of workstations. A system of interconnected PCs is the least expensive configuration of all. The file server can be a powerful, high-speed machine based on the Intel 80386 chip, while the terminals can be 80286-based. Each PC must contain a special add-on board that provides access to the network. Figure 1-4 depicts this configuration.

UNIX and Standards

One of the strongest criticisms of UNIX throughout the years is that it has never been a single, unified product with total compatibility

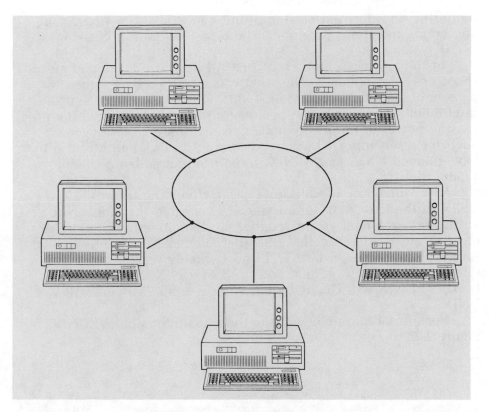

9

Figure 1-4. Personal Computers in a LAN

from one system to another, as DOS has been. The most significant differences have arisen from different versions developed by the three major standard-bearers:

- ▶ AT&T UNIX
- ▶ Microsoft XENIX
- ▶ Berkeley UNIX BSD

The Three Versions

AT&T's System V, the current commercial UNIX for medium-sized and large systems, is derived primarily from AT&T's earlier System III and Version 7, but includes some Berkeley features. System V, Release 3 introduced extensive new communications features, including an improved version of the `uucp` (UNIX-to-UNIX copy and communication) program and a new Remote File Sharing (RFS) system.

In the late 1970s and early 1980s, Microsoft developed an off-shoot of UNIX, called XENIX, that was specifically designed for personal computers. In the late 1980s, with the emergence of the Intel 80386 microprocessor, personal computers now rival the processing power of minicomputers. Because there is no longer a need for a separate UNIX-derived product, AT&T and Microsoft have merged UNIX and XENIX into a product called System V/386, Release 3.2.

The University of California began diverging from AT&T's UNIX in the late 1970s, offering a UNIX system that appeals to scientific research centers, universities, and engineering firms. The most recent release is called BSD (Berkeley standard delivery) 4.3. AT&T plans to merge the AT&T and Berkeley versions in a future release of System V. At that point, AT&T UNIX, XENIX, and Berkeley UNIX will finally be united as a single product called UNIX.

10

For a brief chronology of the three main versions of UNIX, see Figure 1-5.

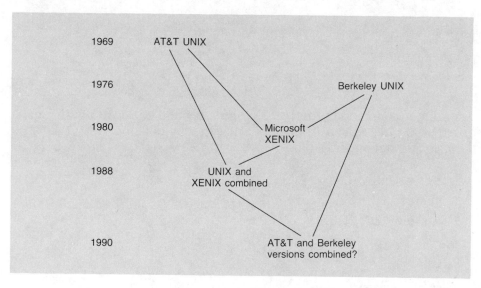

Figure 1-5. The Versions of UNIX

Other Standards

In the area of hardware, a consortium called X/Open has defined a Common Applications Environment (CAE) for computers that run UNIX. Some of the companies actively complying with CAE are Hewlett-Packard, NCR, Unisys, Siemens, Bull, Olivetti, and ICL.

Meanwhile, the Institute of Electrical and Electronic Engineers (IEEE) has also been pressing for a standard for UNIX design called Posix (portable operating system environment standard). Because companies have proliferated so many variations of UNIX, Posix may offer all companies that produce versions of UNIX a means of reaching agreement.

Ever since the introduction of the Macintosh, with its icon-driven graphical user interface, most computer manufacturers have accepted the concept of bit-mapped graphic displays. Such a display is required for both icon-based user interfaces and desktop publishing. To unify the efforts to produce graphic displays for UNIX, some companies have been supporting a standard called X Windows. Their intention is that all bit-mapped displays should adhere to a single standard, just as all character coding now conforms to the standard ASCII.

11

Sun Microsystems and AT&T have announced a user interface called Open Look, which is based on the X Windows and Posix standards. However, DEC, Hewlett-Packard, IBM, and others have formed an Open Software Foundation (OSF), which has responded with a rival user interface of its own. The result is that two graphical interface standards might be established, instead of one.

Getting Started

Now let's consider the basic steps required for you to begin using the UNIX operating system:

Preliminary setup

Logging into the system

Entering commands

Changing your password

Entering commands

Logging out of the system

Preliminary Setup

To help maintain the security of your computer system, you need a *login name* and a *password* to access the UNIX operating system. Each time you log into the system, you must enter your login name; then the system prompts you for a password. Only after you enter the correct password can you use the system.

Your login name may be your first name, your last name, or a combination of the two. If your name is John G. Rogers, then your login name might be one of the following:

john

jgr

rogers

johnr

12

Your password can be up to fourteen characters long. For the protection of the system, it's best to choose a longer password, especially if it includes uppercase letters, numbers, and special characters. With all of these characters, you can invent a password that is easy to remember, yet is difficult for intruders to guess. Following are a few examples:

Don't_4GET_it!

Easy.2.recall

It's-too-late

Laurel&Hardy

In UNIX, most users communicate with the system through a terminal (or a computer in *terminal mode*). If you are using a terminal, your terminal must use communication settings that agree with the settings of the host computer. If your terminal is set incorrectly, one of the following might occur when you attempt to log in:

The screen will be blank

Each character will appear twice

Random characters (called "garbage") will appear on the screen

To correct any of these problems, you must run the `stty` (set terminal) program. This command is discussed in Chapter 8 in the section "Setting Up Terminals."

Logging into the System

After you have a login name, a password, and a correctly set terminal, you can log into your UNIX system. To do so, you must use the following basic steps:

1. Connect your terminal to the system by doing one of the following:
   - ▶ Turn on your terminal.
   - ▶ Press a key (or a combination of keys).
   - ▶ Dial a telephone number through your modem.
   - ▶ The system will respond with the following prompt:
     ```
     login: _
     ```
2. Identify yourself to the system:
   - ▶ Type your login name and press Enter.
   - ▶ The system will respond by prompting for your password:
     ```
     login: larry
     Password: _
     ```

13

3. Enter your password:
   - ▶ Type your password and press Enter.
   - ▶ Your password will not appear on the screen.
   - ▶ Information, such as the following, will appear on your screen:
     ```
     Last login: Wed May 3  09:28:17  on tty07
     UNIX System V, Release 3.2
     $ _
     ```

The dollar sign ($) prompt tells you that the UNIX system is ready to accept a command.

▶ The symbol that actually appears on your screen may be a dollar sign ($), a percent sign (%), or a pound sign (#). This symbol is called the UNIX *shell prompt*. It corresponds to the DOS prompt A> or C>.

Entering Commands

You can type any UNIX command at the shell prompt, and the system will display the result on the screen. Merely type the name of the command and press Enter. Following are a few examples:

To display the date and time, type date and press Enter. This causes UNIX to display the date and time, as in the following example:

```
Thu May 4 08:53:29 PST 1991
```

Note that after the system displays this information, the shell prompt returns.

To find out which users are currently logged in, type who and press Enter. UNIX displays information such as:

```
pat        tty02        May 4    08:51
lee        tty03        May 4    08:23
marie      tty05        May 4    08:04
larry      tty07        May 4    08:53
anne       tty08        May 4    08:19
paul       tty09        May 3    19:28
frog       tty11        May 4    07:47
terry      tty12        May 4    08:39
```

The who display provides the following information:

▶ The login name of each user logged in
▶ The name of the user's terminal (tty*nn*)
▶ The date and time when the user logged in

and then returns you to the shell prompt.

When you type a non-UNIX command, such as sho, and press Enter, UNIX displays the following:

```
sh: sho:  not found
```

Because no such UNIX command exists, an error message appears.

Changing Your Password

When you first start working on a UNIX system, the system administrator usually assigns you a simple password so that you can initially log onto the system. One of the first things you should do after you first log in is to change your password so that it is more difficult for outsiders to guess. On some systems, you are required to change your password periodically. The command for making this change is called `passwd` (note the two missing letters). Use this command as follows:

1. Request a password change:
   ▶ Type `passwd` and press Enter:
   ```
   $ passwd
   Changing password for larry
   Old password: _
   ```
   ▶ Type your current password and press Enter.
2. Enter a new password:
   ▶ Enter your new password:
   ```
   Old password:
   New password:
   Retype your new password: _
   ```
   ▶ Enter your new password again:
   ```
   Retype your new password:
   $ _
   ```

15

▶ Guidelines for selecting a secure password can be found earlier in this chapter, in the section "Preliminary Setup."

Entering a Command Line

Earlier in this chapter, you used the `who` command to list all users currently logged onto the system. If you occasionally work on more than one terminal in a UNIX system, you might need to use a variation of the who command. This who includes an *argument* that modifies the action of the command:

```
$ who am i
larry      tty07      May 4  08:53
$ _
```

Note that UNIX lists the name of the user on the terminal at which the command was typed; it also notes the communication line (tty07) being used.

Most UNIX commands allow you to add arguments that modify the output. Some commands have long lists of arguments too numerous to remember. Commands and arguments are discussed at length in the section "Some Utility Programs" of Chapter 4.

When you are entering a command line, the key combinations that let you erase a single character or erase the entire command line can be helpful. To erase a single character, press one of the following:

16

▶ # (the number sign, or Shift-3)

▶ Hold down the Shift key and press the 3 key at the top of the keyboard.

▶ Ctrl-H (hold down the Ctrl key and press H (or h))
▶ Backspace (a separate key on some keyboards)

Experiment with these combinations to find out which work on your keyboard. Following is an example of how to use the # symbol as the erase key. Let's assume you made a mistake when you meant to type date and actually typed daet:

Press # once to erase the t:

```
$ dae
```
Press # again to erase the e:

```
$ da
```
Type te to correct and press Enter:

```
$ date
Thu May 4 08:53:29 PST 1991
$ _
```

To cancel the command, press the @ (the "at" sign) key
before you press Enter. Following is an example of how to use this
key (referred to as the *kill* key). Let's assume you made a mistake
when you meant to type who am i and actually typed sho am i:

Press @ to erase the entire command line.
Retype the command line and press Enter:

```
who am i
larry      tty07     May 4  08:53
$ _
```

The kill key (@) probably won't erase the command line from
the screen. Instead, the cursor will probably move down to the
next line without displaying a new shell prompt. That is where
you retype the command line.

If you enter a command and nothing happens (it generates no
output and no shell prompt appears), the process might have
"hung up" (failed) in the system. If this ever happens, merely
press the Del key to restore the shell prompt. For example, if you
enter the date command and nothing happens, press Del. The
shell prompt immediately returns to the screen.

17

Logging Out of the System

At the end of a session, you have to *log off* the system. If you
merely turn off your terminal and walk away, UNIX assumes you
are still logged in. If you are paying for time on the system, you
will be billed for the extra time—even though you aren't really
using the system.

The most common way to log out is to press Ctrl-D (hold
down the Ctrl key and press D (or d)). After you've done this, the
login prompt returns to the screen. For example, if you press Ctrl-
D at the shell prompt ($), UNIX does not display the key combina-
tion; it merely clears the screen and displays the following:

```
login:
```

Be sure your screen displays the login prompt before you turn off your terminal. Otherwise, you are still logged onto the system.

▶ On some systems, you may be able to log out by typing `logout` at the shell prompt. After you press Enter, UNIX displays the usual `login:` prompt. This lets you know that you are now disconnected from the system.

What You've Learned

18

This chapter included some general information about UNIX and other operating systems and offered some specific instructions for getting started. In the broadest terms, an operating system is a series of programs that provide a standard working environment which benefits both software developers and everyday users.

DOS and UNIX have some common commands. However, their main difference is that DOS was designed for a single user, while UNIX was designed for many users. In addition, UNIX includes extensive text-processing and text-formatting facilities, along with built-in administrative and development tools.

Typical UNIX configurations include terminals connected to a minicomputer, stand-alone workstations, workstations in a local area network, and PC-based LAN systems.

Historically, UNIX has been plagued with incompatibilities among its different versions, mainly AT&T UNIX, Microsoft XENIX, and Berkeley UNIX. Current efforts are directed at combining the features of the different UNIX packages into a single, standard product. It remains to be seen whether these efforts will be successful.

The chapter includes brief instructions for logging in, using the system, and logging out. To log in, you must have a login name, a password, and a terminal that has been identified and described to the system. After you've logged in, you can begin entering commands at the system shell prompt to perform your work. Merely type a command line, with or without command arguments, and press Enter to perform a function. The command called `passwd` allows you to change your password. At the end of a session, you should always log out of the system before you turn off your terminal.

Chapter 1 Quiz

1. Select the statement that best describes the purpose of an operating system:

    A. To handle file management

    B. To manage the operation of the disk drives

    C. To provide a shell prompt at each user's terminal

    D. To provide a common environment for programmers and users

2. Identify one feature from the following list that is common to both UNIX and DOS:

    A. Commands for creating and deleting directories

    B. Commands for text processing and editing

    C. Commands to facilitate software development

    D. Commands to carry out all aspects of system administration

3. True or false: Personal computers connected in a local area network can form a UNIX system.

4. Which of the following organizations did *not* develop one of the major variations of UNIX?

    A. AT&T

    B. IBM

    C. University of California, Berkeley

    D. Microsoft Corporation

5. Which of the following is *not* required to log in and start using UNIX?

    A. A login name

    B. A password

    C. Knowledge of system administration

    D. A terminal that has been set up to communicate with the host computer

19

6. Which of the following passwords represents a good, sensible choice?

    A. abc

    B. dan

    C. 2B,or.not-2B?

    D. password

7. Which of the following commands would you use to change your password?

    A. `date`

    B. `who`

    C. `who am i`

    D. `passwd`

8. The key that you press to delete the character most recently typed on the command line is called the

    A. Delete key

    B. Erase key

    C. Kill key

    D. Return key

9. The key that you press to delete the entire command line is called the

    A. Kill key

    B. Erase key

    C. Delete key

    D. Return key

10. What combination of keys do you press to log out of the system?

    A. QUIT

    B. OUT

    C. EXIT

    D. Ctrl-D

Chapter 2

The File System

What You Will Learn

This chapter describes the UNIX file system and includes the following topics:

- ▶ Files and directories
- ▶ Types of files
- ▶ Looking at directories
- ▶ Changing directories
- ▶ Creating directories
- ▶ Deleting directories
- ▶ Copying files
- ▶ Renaming and moving files
- ▶ Examining files
- ▶ Deleting files
- ▶ Linking files
- ▶ File permissions

An Overview of the File System

In the UNIX system, as in DOS, text, data, and programs are stored as *files*. Files, in turn, are stored in directories. Files, directories, and the information UNIX uses to keep track of them comprise the *file system*.

Files and Directories

The UNIX system, like DOS, has a file system that is organized in a hierarchical structure. At the top of the hierarchy is the *root directory* (or *root*). Under the root directory are found the major directories. By convention, each UNIX system includes at least five major directories, which have standard names. If you've been using DOS, this is one of the first things you must get used to, because DOS directories don't use standard names.

The names and contents of the five major UNIX directories are summarized in Table 2-1.

Table 2-1. Major UNIX Directories

Name	Contents
usr	User log-in directories for all users who have accounts on the system
bin	Binary files (files used to execute programs)
tmp	Temporary files
dev	Device files (those files that represent the system's terminals, printers, disk drives, tape drives, and so on)
etc	System administration files

Many files *must* reside in specific directories. However, there are always exceptions. On some UNIX systems, directory names may differ from the conventional names; but, aside from minor variations, you can expect to find the five major directories.

The root directory is identified by a slash (/). (Note that below the root directory, a slash indicates another level lower in the file system hierarchy.) The five major directories are identified by the following names (see Figure 2-1):

22

```
/usr
/bin
/tmp
/dev
/etc
```

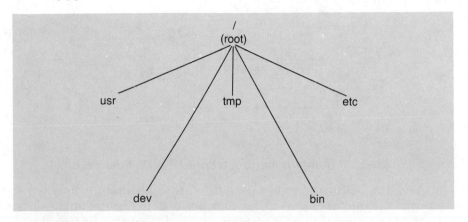

Figure 2-1. The Major Directories

23

A file in directory /usr called alice is identified by the notation /usr/alice. A directory under /etc called passwd is identified by the notation /etc/passwd. A file in /etc/passwd called alice has a *full pathname* called /etc/passwd/alice. The lineage of a file through the various directories above it is called a *path*. The complete name of any file that traces its location in the file system from the root directory is referred to as a full pathname.

A UNIX filename can contain as few as one and as many as 14 characters, excluding slashes (/), question marks (?), asterisks (*), quotation marks (' or "), brackets ([or]), braces ({ or }), or control characters. Unlike a DOS filename, a UNIX filename can include one or more periods in any position in the filename. Another difference is that UNIX distinguishes between uppercase and lowercase letters in filenames. That is, the names REPORT, Report, and report indicate three different filenames in UNIX.

Following are some examples of valid UNIX filenames:

```
news.report
01.week.TEST
interest.rates
f
ABC-123
```

As these examples show, UNIX provides more flexibility than DOS for naming files. Periods, if used, can be placed anywhere in the filename. You are not restricted to a three-character extension following a period, as you are in DOS. (Note the comparison of filenames in Figure 2-2.)

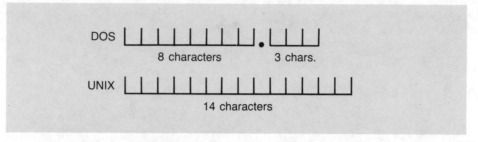

Figure 2-2. A Comparison of DOS and UNIX Filenames

As with DOS, using one period (.) in a pathname represents the current directory, and using two periods (..) represents the parent directory (the directory directly above the current directory).

Types of Files

In the UNIX system, as in DOS, directories are actually files. However, UNIX devices are also represented as files; in this regard, UNIX differs considerably from DOS. DOS has a few fixed device names, such as COM1 (first serial port), LPT1 (first parallel port), and so on, which are directly related to specific hardware devices. However, UNIX lets you access all devices through filenames. Your system can have as many filenames as necessary, and it usually stores the names in a subdirectory of the major directory /dev.

The three types of UNIX files are summarized in Table 2-2.

Table 2-2. Types of Files

Type	Description
Directory file	A file that contains the names of other files (including other directories)
Ordinary file	A file that contains text, data, or programs
Special file	A file that represents a particular hardware device

Handling Directories

A file system is similar to a filing cabinet: A directory is like a drawer in that filing cabinet, and each "drawer" contains individual file folders. The tools described in this section allow you to look at directories, change directories, and create and delete directories.

Looking at Directories *ls*

The ls (list) command displays the contents of a directory; thus, the UNIX ls command is similar to the DOS dir command. When you use ls without any options, it displays only the filenames in the current directory, as in the following example:

```
$ ls
answers
bates.file
call_FILES
ddd-125
zero+one
$ _
```

25

This simple directory listing doesn't distinguish between ordinary files and directories. It also doesn't display any information about individual files. To access this additional information, request a *long* listing by adding –l (hyphen el) to the basic ls command, as follows:

```
$ ls -l
total 10
drwx--x---   2   paul   258   Jul 18   15:42   answers
-rwxr-x---   1   paul    92   Feb 20   09:14   bates.file
drwx--x---   1   paul   126   Nov 31   08:57   call_FILES
-rw-r-----   3   paul   415   Aug  3   13:09   ddd-125
-rw-r-----   1   paul   361   May 11   10:38   zero+one
$ _
```

▶ If you want to use an option with a command, always
  insert a space between the command name and the
option (or options).

This display includes seven major columns of information. Figure 2-3 illustrates the meaning of each of these columns.

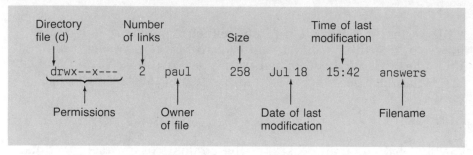

Figure 2-3. Information in a Long Listing

Let's review the information shown in Figure 2-3. The first column of the display contains ten characters. The first character indicates whether the file is an ordinary file (-) or a directory (d). The remaining nine characters indicate file permissions (discussed in the "File Permissions" section of this chapter).

The number in the second column is the number of *links* in the file system to this file (discussed under "Linking Files" later in this chapter). The name in the third column is the *owner* of the file (the user who originally created the file). The number in the fourth column is the size of the file in characters (or bytes).

The fifth and sixth columns give the date and time when the file was last modified. Finally, the seventh column gives the name of the file itself.

Changing Directories   *cd*

The UNIX command for changing directories has the same name as the DOS command—`cd`. When you first log into UNIX, you are located in your *home directory*. You can change to one of your own subdirectories and work in it at any time. If you have permission, you can also move to other users' directories and work there.

A common use of the `cd` command is to change from the current directory to the parent directory. To do this, use the command:

```
$ cd ..
$ _
```

26

The parent directory is now your working (current) directory. In DOS, the `PROMPT $P` command displays the name of your current directory; in UNIX, the `pwd` (print working directory) command displays the pathname. The following example uses `pwd` before and after changing directories (see Figure 2-4):

```
$ pwd
/usr/allen
$ cd letters
$ pwd
/usr/allen/letters
$ _
```

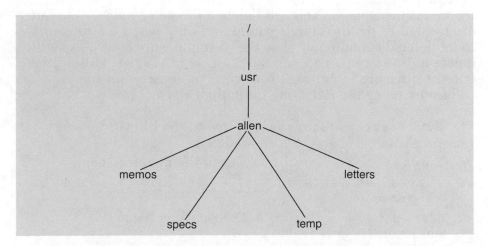

Figure 2-4. Changing Directories

Creating a Directory   *mkdir*

The UNIX `mkdir` (make directory) command works exactly like the DOS `md` (or `mkdir`) command. When you need a new directory, move to the directory under which you want it created, and use the command `mkdir` *new_directory*, as in the following example:

```
$ cd letters
$ mkdir plans
$ _
```

The commands in this example create a new subdirectory (called `plans`) under `letters`.

UNIX directories, like DOS directories, help you organize your work. Instead of accumulating all your files in one large directory, you can group your files by project or subject matter in different directories.

Deleting a Directory   *rmdir*

If you no longer need a directory, you can remove it from the file system with the `rmdir` command, which works like the DOS `rd` (or `rmdir`) command. You can delete a directory only when you are located in the directory's parent and only when the directory to be deleted contains no files. For example, suppose you want to delete a directory named `/usr/allen/letters/storage`. If your current directory is `/usr/allen`, you could carry out the procedure by using the following individual steps:

28

`$ cd /letters/storage`	Move to the directory being deleted

`$ pwd`
`/usr/allen/letters`
`/storage`
	Check the directory name

`$ rm -i *` old.letter: ? old.memo: ? old.study: ?	Delete all its files
`$ cd ..`	Move to the parent directory
`$ rmdir storage`	Delete the directory $ _

Handling Files

Most of the work you do with a computer involves manipulating files. Some of the more common operations you perform are creating new files, examining files, deleting old files, and moving files around.

Copying Files   *cp*

The copy command in UNIX is called cp. To use this command, type cp, the name of the original file, and then the name of the target (new) file. For example, the following command:

```
$ cp old.file new.file
$ _
```

makes a copy of old.file called new.file.

 This example illustrates a common ordering of UNIX commands: *command previous next*

29

You can use cp to copy one or more files from the current directory to another, as shown in the following example:

```
$ cp memo letter report ../papers
$ _
```

This example copies the files memo, letter, and report from the current directory to another directory under the same parent directory called papers. This is shown in Figure 2-5. (Note that the files retain their names in the new directory.)

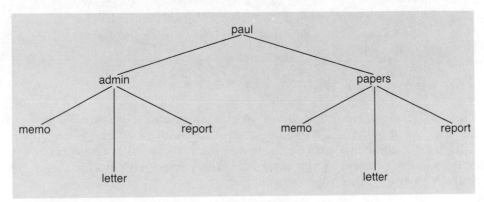

Figure 2-5. Copying Files to Another Directory

If you are copying a single file from one directory to another, you can give the file a new name in the other directory. The following example copies the file old.file to the directory papers and renames it new.file:

```
$ cp old.file ../papers /new.file
$ _
```

Examining Files   *cat*

The UNIX cat (concatenate) command, like the DOS type command, displays the contents of a file on the screen. Following is an example of its usage:

```
$ cat memo
This is a reminder
about Thursday's
meeting at 3:00.
$ _
```

30

If you misspell the name of the file, or if no such file exists, the only output UNIX generates is an error message, as in the following example. (Note that you can use cat as a fast way to find out whether or not a file exists.)

```
$ cat memmo
cat: cannot open memmo
$ _
```

Thus, file memmo does not exist in the current directory.

The other major function of this command—concatenation—is discussed in Chapter 4.

Renaming and Moving Files   *mv*

The UNIX mv (move) command works somewhat like the DOS rename command to give a file a new name. To rename a file (or directory), the safest procedure is to check to see that the target name doesn't already exist, and only then make the change, as shown in the following example:

```
$ cat new.file
cat: cannot open new.file
$ mv old.file new.file
$ _
```

You use the `cat` command to make sure that `new.file` isn't already the name of a file. If it isn't (UNIX returns an error message), then you can proceed to change the name of `old.file` to `new.file`—without having to worry about overwriting an existing file.

▶ The previous example illustrates one of the characteristics of the UNIX system: It doesn't include the safeguards and conveniences that many application programs include. When you use `mv`, UNIX doesn't offer a prompt to protect you, such as: `"A file with that name already exists. Do you want to overwrite the file? (Y/N)."` With UNIX, you usually have to provide your own safeguards.

31

As its name implies, the other major function of `mv` is to move files from the current directory to another. In the following example, you will be moving files `ltr.101`, `ltr.102`, and `ltr.103` from the current directory to directory `letters` (see Figure 2-6):

```
$ mv ltr.101 ltr.102 ltr.103 ../letters
$ _
```

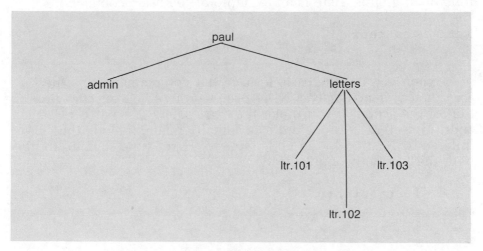

Figure 2-6. Moving Files to Another Directory

In the previous example, `letters` is another subdirectory whose parent is the same directory as that of the current directory. You could use the `ls` command to confirm the move, as follows:

```
$ ls ../letters
ltr.101
ltr.102
ltr.103
[elp]
$ _
```

When you move a single file, you can also rename it, as shown in the following example:

```
$ mv ltr.104 ../letters/conference
$ _
```

32

In the previous example you are changing the name of `ltr.104` to `conference` while moving it to the directory `letters`. Again, you could use `ls` to confirm the move and name change.

Deleting Files   *rm*

The `rm` (remove) command lets you delete files, either one at a time or in groups. Here is an example of the basic command:

```
$ rm memo test
$ _
```

When you use the basic form of the `rm` command, the files are deleted immediately; UNIX doesn't prompt you for confirmation of the action. If you prefer the extra safety of having to confirm each deletion before it is actually made, include the −i (interactive) option to the `rm` command. Here is the same example with the interactive option added:

```
$ rm -i memo test
memo: ?
test: ?
$ _
```

When you request confirmation in this way, UNIX displays each filename one at a time with a question mark. At each line, type either y to confirm the deletion or n to prevent the file from being deleted.

Linking Files   *ln*

A group of users on the same UNIX system can *share* a file while working on a joint project. Sharing the file allows any of the users to update the file at any time. One user can modify the file at 1:17; then another user can modify it at 2:03. If a third user displays the file at 2:34, the third user sees the changes made by the previous two users.

UNIX makes file-sharing possible by providing *links* to any existing file. Each link to the file is simply another name by which the file is known to another user in another directory. Although only one file exists on the system, each link makes the file accessible to another user on the system.

Consider the following situation: Lisa and Paul are both working on a project that requires the use of file results, which is located in Lisa's sales directory. Paul wants to access file results from his own directory, named support. He can obtain access to results by executing the ln (link) command from his directory support, as follows:

```
$ cd support
$ ln /usr/lisa/sales/results progress
$ _
```

After executing these commands, Paul now has access to the file results from his own directory support. Notice that Paul has renamed the file as progress (but he could have retained the name results). The link between files and directories is illustrated in Figure 2-7.

After working on the file, Paul can always remove the link by using the rm command, as follows:

```
$ pwd
/usr/paul/support
$ rm progress
$ _
```

33

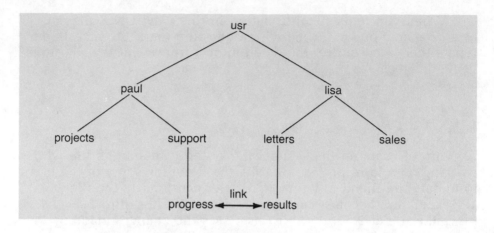

Figure 2-7. A Link to a File Called `results`

34

    With this command, Paul removes his own link to the file, but not the original file in Lisa's directory.

Matching Characters

When you are working with UNIX files, you can use *wildcard* characters to help select filenames. Two of the wildcard characters used in UNIX—the question mark (?) and the asterisk (*)—are also used in DOS. As in DOS, the question mark is used to match a single character, and the asterisk is used to match any number of characters. In UNIX, however, you can also enumerate specific characters to be matched between a pair of brackets. These three wildcard selectors are summarized in Table 2-3.

Table 2-3. Wildcard Symbols

Symbol	Meaning
?	Match any single character in the position of the symbol
*	Match any number of characters in the position of the symbol
[xxx]	Match the specific characters typed between the brackets

    Let's assume you have three files named `memo.1`, `memo.2`, and `memo.3`. You could use the following command to copy them to a directory called `MEMOS`:

```
$ cp memo.? ../MEMOS
$ _
```

To delete these files from the current directory, you could use the following command:

```
$ rm memo.?
$ _
```

If you had three files called `test.c`, `algorithm.c`, and `abstract.c`, you could move them to directory `c_progs` with the following command:

```
$ mv *.c ../c_progs
$ _
```

In UNIX, a third type of wildcard notation lets you narrow the match to a set of specified characters. For example, suppose your directory contains the following nine files:

```
test.1    test.2    test.3
test.4    test.5    test.6
test.7    test.8    test.9
```

To delete only the three files in the middle column, you could include their suffix numbers within brackets, as follows:

```
$ rm test.[258]
$ _
```

This command is equivalent to the following expanded command:

```
$ rm test.2 test.5 test.8
$ _
```

For consecutive numbers (or letters), such as those in the filenames in the middle row, you can use a hyphen in the brackets to indicate a range, as shown in the following command:

```
$ rm test.[4-6]
$ _
```

This command is equivalent to the following expanded command:

```
$ rm test.4 test.5 test.6
$ _
```

File Permissions

A system administrator for a UNIX system can maintain a measure of security among its users through a system of file permissions, which determine who may or may not read or use a given file. All files (including all directories) are assigned permissions, which apply to the individual user, to any *group* to which the user belongs, and to all other users on the system. We'll begin with a discussion of how to read the symbolic representation of permissions, then consider how to change permissions for a file.

Reading Permissions   *ls -l*

Earlier in this chapter, you saw the display created by the "long listing" option of the ls command:

```
$ ls -l
total 10
drwx--x---   2   paul   258   Jul 18   15:42   answers
-rwxr-x---   1   paul    92   Feb 20   09:14   bates.file
drwx--x---   1   paul   126   Nov 31   08:57   call_FILES
-rw-r-----   3   paul   415   Aug  3   13:09   ddd-125
-rw-r-----   1   paul   361   May 11   10:38   zero+one
$ _
```

The first column of the long listing includes ten characters. The first character, as noted earlier, denotes the type of file:

-       Ordinary file
d   Directory

The next nine characters give a symbolic representation of the permissions currently in effect for the file. These nine characters

36

are actually three columns of three characters each, even though they are not separated by spaces. The first column represents the user, the second represents the user's working group (if the user belongs to a group), and the third represents all other users on the system. Let's look at the files permission column of the ls –l display and add spaces to make it easier to read. The listing would now look like this:

Type	User	Group	Others	Name
d	rwx	--x	---	answers
-	rwx	r-x	---	bates.file
d	rwx	--x	---	call_FILES
-	rw-	r--	---	ddd-125
-	rw-	r--	---	zero+one

Each of the three permission groups contains three characters. These represent permission to read (**r**), permission to write (**w**), permission to execute (**x**), and permission denied (**-**). The meanings of the permissions differ somewhat for files and directories, as shown in Table 2-4.

37

Table 2-4. Explanation of Permissions

Permission	Meaning for a File	Meaning for a Directory
Read	Look at the contents	View the list of filenames
Write	Change the contents	Add files to and remove files from the directory
Execute	Use the filename as a UNIX command	Change to the directory, search the directory, and copy files from it

Let's single out one of the lines from the previous ls –l display and read the permissions from left to right:

```
—        rwx       r-x      ---        bates.file
```

After the first hyphen, which indicates that this is an ordinary file, the nine permissions symbols are as follows:

The **owner** of bates.file can:

r read the file
w write to (change) the file
x execute the file

Other members of the   r read the file
owner's working **group** can: - not write to the file
                            x execute the file

All other users are denied   - no reading
access to the file: - no writing
                            - no executing

Changing Permissions   *chmod*

You can use the chmod (change [access] mode) command to change permissions for any files that you have created. If you are the owner of a file, the chmod command lets you use the + symbol on the command line to add new permissions and use the – symbol to remove existing permissions. The command also lets you use the = symbol to assign permissions *absolutely*, which means that you replace all existing permissions with a completely new set of permissions.

For example, to allow the other members of your working group (**g**) to write to bates.file, you would execute the following command:

```
$ chmod g+w bates.file
$ _
```

You can use ten different symbols to change permissions on a chmod command line. These symbols are summarized in Table 2-5. Each change requires you to choose one of the symbols from the first column, one from the second column, and at least one from the third column.

Table 2-5. Symbols for chmod

Users Affected	Action Requested	Permission
u owner (user)	+ add permission	r to read
g group	– remove permission	w to write
o all others	= absolute permission	x to execute
a all users (default)		

To change permissions for more than one class of users, you can include additional change requests on one command line. Merely separate each change from the others with a comma, with no space before or after the comma. For example, to add write permission to members of your working group and also add read and write permissions to all other users, execute the following command:

```
$ chmod g+w,o+rw bates.file
$ _
```

To display the result of this command very clearly, you could use ls –l (specifying one file) before and after you execute chmod. Then you can see the permissions displayed before and after the change. This is how it would look:

```
$ ls -l bates.file
-rwxr-x---  1  paul        92  Feb 20  09:14  bates.file
$ chmod g+w,o+rw bates.file
$ ls -l bates.file
-rwxrgxrw-  1  paul        92  Feb 20  09:14  bates.file
$ _
```

39

To revoke permissions currently in effect, use a minus sign instead of a plus sign. The following example shows you how to revoke the permissions that were granted in the previous example:

```
$ ls -l bates.file
-rwxrwxrw-  1  paul        92  Feb 20  09:14  bates.file
$ chmod g-w,o-rw bates.file
$ ls -l bates.file
-rwxr-x---  1  paul        92  Feb 20  09:14  bates.file
$ _
```

An alternate approach to granting or revoking permissions is to use the equal sign (=) to clear all current permissions and set new ones. For example, suppose you decide to revoke all permissions for bates.file, but you want to reset permission to read and write for yourself and permission to read for your group. You can accomplish this by using the following series of commands:

```
$ ls -l bates.file
-rwxr-x---  1  paul        92  Feb 20  09:14  bates.file
$ chmod u=rw,g=r,o= bates.file
$ ls -l bates.file
-rw-r-----  1  paul        92  Feb 20  09:14  bates.file
```

▶ A word of caution about the chmod command: Be careful when you use this command. You can lock yourself out of your own files if you make a mistake with chmod. For example, the command:

$ chmod u=,g=,o=

makes a file inaccessible to *all* users, including yourself.

What You've Learned

40

This chapter described files and directories. You learned that directories are files that name other files and act as storage locations. The three types of files are directories, ordinary files, and special files (which represent hardware devices).

The section about directories taught you how to use the following commands: ls to display the contents of a directory (with or without detailed information), cd to change directories, pwd to display the name of the current directory, mkdir to create a directory, and rmdir to delete a directory.

The section about files taught you how to use the following commands: cat to display the contents of a file, cp to copy files, mv to rename and move files, and ln to create a link to a file. These commands can all be used with the wildcard characters ? (match any character), * (match any number of characters), [xxx] (match the characters specified between the brackets).

The section about file permissions showed you how to use the following commands: ls –l to display permissions and chmod to change permissions.

Chapter 2 Quiz

Match each command listed on the left with one of the tasks described on the right:

1. `cat file.101`	A. Display the names of all files in the current directory (without any other information).
2. `rm memo.101`	B. Display the names of all files in the current directory (along with permissions, size, and date and time of last change).
3. `cd ../NOTES`	C. Change to directory `NOTES`.
4. `ls -l`	D. Create a new directory called `NOTES`.
5. `cp memo.101 memo.102`	E. Delete directory `NOTES` (assuming that it is already empty).
6. `ls`	F. Display the contents of `file.101`.
7. `mkdir NOTES`	G. Make a copy of `memo.101` called `memo.102`.
8. `ln ...memo.101 memo.101`	H. Add write permission for other users for file `memo.101`.
9. `chmod o+w memo.101`	I. Delete file `memo.101`.
10. `rmdir NOTES`	J. Add a link to file `memo.101`.
11. `mv memo.101 memo.102`	K. Move file `memo.101` to directory `NOTES`.
12. `mv memo.101 ../NOTES`	L. Change the name of file `memo.101` to `memo.102`.

41

Using the partial diagram of the file system shown below in Figure 2-8 write a command line to accomplish each of the following tasks:

13. Lisa: Copy files `memo.1`, `memo.2`, `memo.3`, and `memo.4` from the directory `sales` to the directory `MEMOS`. (Assume you are now in `sales`.)

14. Paul: Change from the directory `projects` to the directory `paul`.

15. Lisa: Move files `personnel.G`, `materials.G`, and `expenses.G` from the directory `letters` to the directory `sales`. (Assume that these are the only files in the directory `letters` that end with the suffix `.G`.)

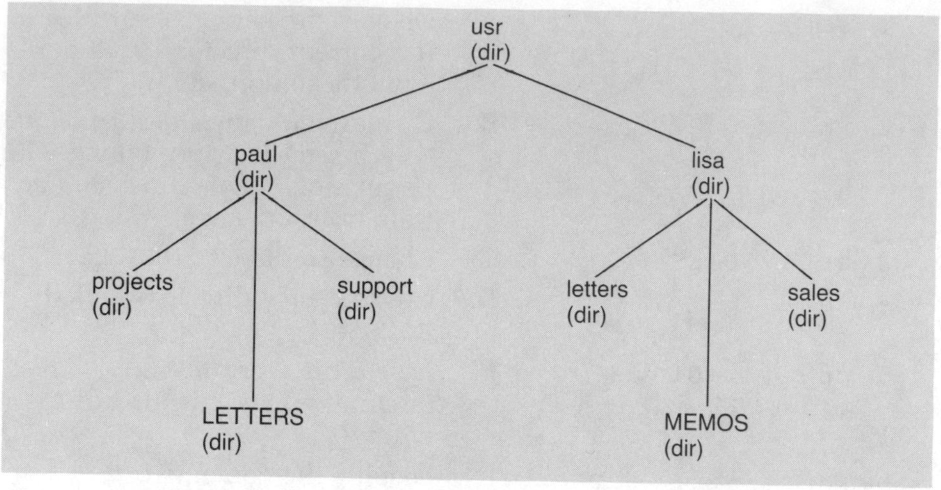

Figure 2-8. A Sample File System

42

16. Paul: Display the permissions of all files in directory `support`. (Assume you are now in `support`.)

17. Lisa: Add a link in your current working directory (`letters`) to a file called `expedite` in Paul's directory `LETTERS`, using the same name for the file.

18. Paul: In your home directory, create a new subdirectory called `news`.

19. Lisa: Make the following changes to permissions for file `meeting` in the directory `sales`: grant permission to execute to yourself; grant permission to write to members of your working group; revoke permission to read, write, and execute to all other users. (Assume you are now in directory `sales`.)

20. Paul: Delete the following files from directory `LETTERS`: `interest.K`, `interest.N`, and `interest.R`. (Assume that you have 26 files that end with the suffix `.K` in this directory.)

Chapter 3
Processing Commands

What You Will Learn

When you have a job to do in UNIX, you use a *command*. Every command that you enter is executed by the UNIX command processor, called the *shell*. The resulting operation is called a *process*. This chapter shows you how the UNIX shell processes (executes) commands and how you can use various shell features to modify UNIX commands. You will learn the following:

- ► How to construct a command line
- ► How to redirect input and output of commands
- ► How to connect processes with pipes and tees
- ► How to execute commands in the background
- ► How to create simple shell scripts
- ► How to change key shell values

The Different Shell Programs

The original command processor, which was developed at AT&T by Stephen R. Bourne in the early 1970s, is known as the *Bourne shell*. This is the official shell that is distributed with UNIX systems. The Bourne shell is the fastest UNIX command processor available.

Another command processor, developed by William Joy and others at the University of California in the mid-1970s, is known as the *C shell*. This program, which borrows many concepts from the C language, offers greater versatility than the Bourne shell; its main drawback is its slower execution. Although not considered to be part of System V, the C shell is nearly always available as an alternate command processor. In fact, as soon as you request a login account, the first thing the system administrator usually asks you is which shell you prefer. (For detailed information about the C shell, see Appendix C.)

A third command processor, developed by David Korn in the early 1980s, is called the *Korn shell*. This program combines many of the best features of the two earlier command processors, and it is gaining in popularity. (AT&T may adopt the Korn shell as its official shell some time in the 1990s.) Because few systems offer the Korn shell, we'll restrict our discussion to the Bourne and C shells.

44

Most of the features described in this chapter are supported by all the different command processors. One difference between the Bourne and C shells is that the default shell prompt uses different symbols:

Bourne Shell	C Shell
$ _	% _

Any features unique to the C shell are noted later in this chapter. The default shell prompts identify examples for the two shell programs.

Commands and Command Lines

The Shell Prompt

After you log in, the command processor, or shell, displays a prompt on the screen:

$ _

This *shell prompt*, which is similar to the DOS prompt C>, tells you that the shell is ready to accept input in the form of a *command line*. A command line includes the name of a command, any command options that you want to add, and the name(s) of any file(s) to be processed. Every command line must include the name of a command; command options and filenames may or may not be required.

Entering a Command Line

As you learned in Chapter 2, a command like `ls` (list the contents of a directory) can be entered without a single option or filename, as shown here:

```
$ ls
answers
bates.file
call_FILES
ddd-125
zero+one
$ _
```

45

However, you can also enter an `ls` command line that includes an option, like `-l` (long listing):

```
$ ls -l
total 10
drwx--x---  2  paul      258  Jul 18  15:42  answers
-rwxr-x---  1  paul       92  Feb 20  09:14  bates.file
drwx--x---  1  paul      126  Nov 31  08:57  call_FILES
-rw-r-----  3  paul      415  Aug  3  13:09  ddd-125
-rw-r-----  1  paul      361  May 11  10:38  zero+one
$ _
```

A third variation executed from a different directory, includes a filename (actually a directory name):

```
$ ls /usr/roger/misc
answers
bates.file
call_FILES
ddd-125
zero+one
$ _
```

Finally, a fourth variation, also executed from a different directory, includes both the option and the directory name:

```
$ ls -l /usr/roger/misc
total 10
drwx--x---   2   paul      258   Jul 18   15:42   answers
-rwxr-x---   1   paul       92   Feb 20   09:14   bates.file
drwx--x---   1   paul      126   Nov 31   08:57   call_FILES
-rw-r-----   3   paul      415   Aug  3   13:09   ddd-125
-rw-r-----   1   paul      361   May 11   10:38   zero+one
$ _
```

Command Arguments

46

The –l option and the filename are referred to collectively as *arguments*. Arguments on a command line modify the way the command works. The –l option is one of 22 options supported by the ls command. A few of the other options include –t (sort entries by the time of their last modification), –u (sort entries by the time of their last access), –s (sort entries by their size), and –r (list entries in reverse order).

Each command line, which always includes a command name and may or may not include command arguments, can be described by the following generic representation. (Note that the brackets indicate optional items on the command line. Do not type these characters as part of the command line.)

$ *name* [*options*] [*files*]

in which

> *name* is the command name
>
> *options* represents one or more command options
>
> *files* represents one or more filenames (including directory names)

As shown above, options precede filenames on a command line. If you must use more than one filename, list the names in order (from first to last or from *source* to *target*).

Commands and Processes

New users are often perplexed by the distinction between a command and a process. Here is a brief clarification. A command names a program file, which is stored in a directory on disk. A process is a sequence of actions that take place in memory after a command has been executed. A command is static; a process is active. A command represents potential action; a process is the realization of that potential.

Redirection of Input and Output

In the previous section, each example of the 1s command shows the basic elements of processes: *input* (the command line), *processing* of the input, and *output* (the listing of filenames). The output is the result of the processing. These actions are illustrated in Figure 3-1.

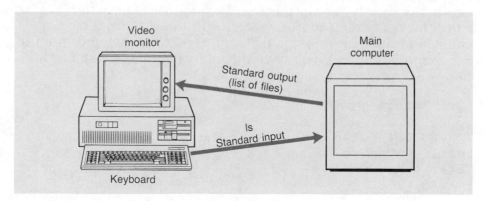

Figure 3-1. Standard Input and Output

You ordinarily enter input from your keyboard and display output on your video screen. To the UNIX system, your keyboard is the *standard input* and your video screen is the *standard output*. However, many commands let you *redirect* the input or output. On the one hand, you can have the shell receive input from a file instead of from the keyboard. On the other hand, you can have the shell send output to a printer instead of to the screen.

47

The symbols used to request redirection are the less than sign (<) and the greater than sign (>):

<   Redirects input from the file (including a device) named on the right

>   Redirects output to the file (including a device) named on the right

 You can think of these symbols as arrows pointing in the direction of the flow of text during processing.

Redirection of Input

48

In Chapter 6, you will learn about the `mail` command, which allows you to send a message to another user via electronic mail. Ordinarily, you type your message from the keyboard after you enter the `mail` command. However, with the aid of redirection, you can also send a message that you have already stored in a file. For example, suppose you have the following message stored in a file called `meeting`:

```
$ cat meeting

I need the notes you took at last month's
meeting. Can you send me a copy some time
later this week?
$ _
```

To send this message to John via electronic mail, you would enter the following command line:

```
$ mail john < meeting
```

The redirection symbol (<) tells the shell to receive its input from file `meeting` rather than from the keyboard. The shell locates file `meeting`, reads the message, and forwards it to the user named John. This is illustrated in Figure 3-2.

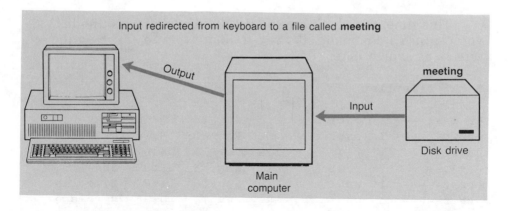

Figure 3-2. Redirection of Input

Redirection of Output

Earlier in this chapter, you saw four variations of the ls command
used to display the contents of a directory. In each instance, the
list was displayed on the screen. However, by using redirection,
you could send the list to a file instead. For important information, storing the output in a file gives you a permanent record
rather than merely a fleeting screen display. Following is an example of a command line that illustrates redirection of the output of
a process (illustrated in Figure 3-3):

49

```
$ ls -l > file.list
$ _
```

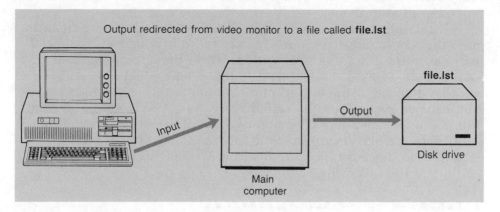

Figure 3-3. Redirection of Output

This time, you don't see the list displayed. To see the list, you can use a command like cat to display file.list on the screen, as shown here:

```
$ cat file.list
total 12
drwx--x---   2   paul      258   Jul 18   15:42   answers
-rwxr-x---   1   paul       92   Feb 20   09:14   bates.file
drwx--x---   1   paul      126   Nov 31   08:57   call_FILES
-rw-r-----   3   paul      415   Aug  3   13:09   ddd-125
-rw-r-----   1   paul        0   Sep 12   11:24   file.list
-rw-r-----   1   paul      361   May 11   10:38   zero+one
$ _
```

If you want to collect a series of lists in a single file, you can use a variation of the redirection symbol to *append* a new list to an existing file. For example, suppose you want to store lists of the contents of three subdirectories (first, second, and third) in a file named dirs.123, which is stored in the parent directory. To do so, you would execute the following sequence:

```
$ ls -l first > ../dirs.123
$ ls -l second >> ../dirs.123
$ ls -l third >> ../dirs.123
$ _
```

The ordinary symbol (>) is used for the first directory; then the symbol for appending text (>>) is used for the second and third directories. Consequently, dirs.123 contains all three lists in consecutive order.

If the target file doesn't exist, either symbol (> or >>) creates a new file. If the target file already exists, the ordinary symbol (>) will cause the file to be overwritten, while the append symbol (>>) will merely append the new text to the existing text.

To dispose of the output of a command, rather than save it, you can redirect it to a file called /dev/null. This special device file is the UNIX system's version of a "wastebasket"—any output sent there merely disappears and never reaches your screen. For example, to discard older articles from Usenet (Chapter 6), you could use the following command:

```
$ readnews -p -n all > /dev/null
$ _
```

50

Connecting Processes

You can make your commands more efficient by connecting processes directly, rather than redirecting the output of one process to a file and then redirecting the input of another process from that file.

Using Pipes

Another way to control the flow of processing is to have the shell connect two processes with a *pipe*. When you use a pipe, the output of one process becomes the input of another. The pipe eliminates the need for intermediary files that temporarily hold the results of one process until you use them in another process. (These files eventually have to be deleted when you finish your operation.)

The symbol for a pipe is a vertical bar (¦), which you enter between the command names on the command line. For example, suppose that you want to print three files called ch.1, ch.2, and ch.3. Rather than print each one separately with the lp command, you can concatenate and print the files with a single command line, as follows:

```
$ cat ch.1 ch.2 ch.3 ¦ lp
request id is epson-143 (1 file)
$ _
```

As the sample system message indicates, the lp command handled only one file because the three files were concatenated by cat before they reached lp. This example of a pipe is illustrated in Figure 3-4.

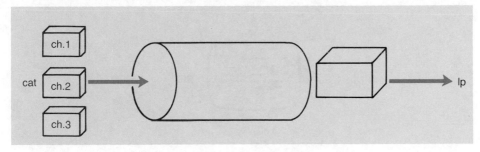

Figure 3-4. An Example of a Pipe

51

Using Tees

The tee command, which is used in conjunction with a pipe, allows you to write text to a file while simultaneously displaying it on your video screen. This is a remarkably handy command, because it combines the advantages of viewing text and storing it in a file. In the following example, you display the contents of a directory and write the list to a file called dir.files:

```
$ ls -l ¦ tee dir.list
total 10
drwx--x---   2   paul    258   Jul 18   15:42   answers
-rwxr-x---   1   paul     92   Feb 20   09:14   bates.file
drwx--x---   1   paul    126   Nov 31   08:57   call_FILES
-rw-r-----   3   paul    415   Aug  3   13:09   ddd-125
-rw-r-----   1   paul    361   May 11   10:38   zero+one
$ _
```

52

With this command line, which is illustrated in Figure 3-5, you get an immediate display and also a file that you can refer back to at your leisure.

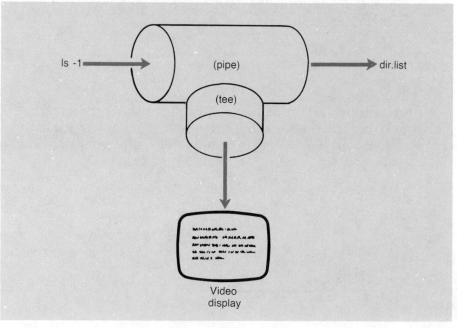

Figure 3-5. An Example of a Tee

After you've executed the previous `tee` command, you can retrieve the listing at any time. Merely display the contents of `dir.list`, as follows:

```
$ cat dir.list
total 10
drwx--x---   2   paul        258  Jul 18  15:42   answers
-rwxr-x---   1   paul         92  Feb 20  09:14   bates.file
drwx--x---   1   paul        126  Nov 31  08:57   call_FILES
-rw-r-----   3   paul        415  Aug  3  13:09   ddd-125
-rw-r-----   1   paul        361  May 11  10:38   zero+one
$ _
```

Since the `tee` command sends output to the video screen, you can request additional processing for this output. For example, referring to the previous example, suppose all you wanted to display on the screen was the entry for the file that included `ddd` in its name. To do so, you could pipe the previous output to the `grep` command (a text-searching command that is described in detail in the next chapter). The new command line would look like this:

```
$ ls -l | tee dir.files | grep ddd
-rw-r-----   3   paul        415  Aug  3  13:09   ddd-125
$ _
```

This command generates a complete listing of your files in `dir.files` and also immediately displays the entry for the file `ddd-125`. (If you had other files that included `ddd` in their names, their entries would also have been displayed.)

Background Processing

One of the features of UNIX that distinguishes it from DOS is its capacity for *multitasking*. Multitasking makes it possible for each user to have more than one process active in the system at any one moment. With multitasking, you could, for example, initiate the formatting of a large file, and then immediately begin editing another file. Formatting would take place as a *background* process, while editing would proceed as a *foreground* process. Background processing relinquishes the screen immediately, while foreground processing requires user interaction and doesn't allow you to start another process.

Requesting a Background Process   &

The symbol used to request background processing is the ampersand (&), which you type at the end of the command line. Following is an example of its usage:

```
$ nroff -cm ch. 5 | lp &
289
$ vi ch.6
```

54

In this example, you begin formatting ch.5 with the nroff command, and then immediately begin editing ch.6 without waiting for the previous process to complete. The shell initiates the formatting process, the *kernel* assigns a process number (289), and then it returns control of the screen to you. If you ever need to terminate the background process, you must refer to it by this number. (See "Terminating a Background Process" later in this chapter.)

> ▶ The *kernel* is the program that interacts directly with the hardware. As a new user, you will rarely be aware of the operations of the kernel.

When you perform background processing, you have to be careful that the background process and the foreground process don't interfere with each other. Any screen output from the background process could disrupt the screen in the middle of your work with the foreground process. In the previous example, when nroff processing is completed and the text is piped to lp, the lp command displays a message on the screen such as the following:

```
request id is epson-132 (1 file)
```

This message writes over your current screen display, but it does not change anything in the foreground file. Merely clear the message and resume work in vi, the UNIX text editor. (The command to clear a message like this is Ctrl-L.)

Messages like this are relatively harmless, but you don't want the actual output from the background process displayed on the screen. To avoid this, merely redirect the output from all background processes that would ordinarily send output to the screen. Because the output of lp is sent to a printer, this example requires no redirection.

Checking on Background Processes *ps*

Sometimes you will need to check on a background process to determine its current status. Is it still running? Has it completed? Or did it run into problems? The ps (process status) command generates a one-line entry for each of your processes that is currently active. The following display shows the active processes in the previous example:

55

```
$ ps
PID        TTY        TIME       COMMAND
289        05         0:03       nroff ch.5
291        05         0:04       vi ch.6
052        05         0:29       -sh
301        05         0:01       -ps
$ _
```

These four columns display the following information: the process identifier (PID), your current terminal number (TTY), the length of time each process has been active, in minutes and seconds (TIME), and the name of the command (COMMAND). The process number of the background formatting job (289) appears at the top of the list, indicating that it has started. In the COMMAND column, note that the shell (-sh) and the process status command (-ps) are listed with your other processes. If you use the ps command, but don't find your background process listed in the display, the process may be completed already.

Terminating a Background Process *kill*

If you ever need to terminate a background process, you can use the kill command to do the job. This command requires one argument—the process identifier (PID), which is first displayed when you start a background process and later when you use the ps command. The following command terminates the formatting job in the previous examples:

```
$ kill 289
$ _
```

Unfortunately, the kill command doesn't report any results. The only way to determine whether or not your request has been successful is to run ps again, as follows:

```
$ ps
PID        TTY         TIME        COMMAND
289        05          0:07        nroff ch.5
291        05          0:08        vi ch.6
052        05          0:33        -sh
301        05          0:01        -ps
$ _
```

56

If ps indicates that your process is still active, as it does in this display, then you must use a more effective version of the command. You can run kill again with the -9 option, which specifies that kill cannot be ignored by the target process. Use this command as follows:

```
$ kill -9 289
$ _
```

The -9 option is more powerful, but also riskier. If the process identifier in this instance is either 0 or 52 (the process number of your shell), you will automatically log yourself out.

Executing Commands from Files

If you are used to working with DOS, then you are probably familiar with the concept of a batch file: you store a sequence of commands in a file; then you execute the file as if it were a command to cause the entire sequence to be carried out. You can do something very similar in UNIX with a *shell program* (also referred to as a *shell script* or *shell file*). The main difference is that a shell script lets you use much more sophisticated constructions than a batch file. However, this chapter will introduce only the simpler techniques.

Obtaining Directory Information

Suppose you'd like to set up an executable file that would do the following three things:

Display the date and time
Display the name of the current directory
Display the contents of the current directory

You also want to run this sequence each time you enter a new directory. To do so, you need only to enter three lines into a file and then make the file executable. You can create the file and enter the command lines by using the cat command, as follows:

57

```
$ cat > dir.look
date
pwd
ls -l
Ctrl-D
$ _
```

In DOS, you have to give each batch file a certain extension to its name (BAT). In UNIX, you can use any legal file name, but you have to remember to make the file executable. In this example, you do this by using the following command:

```
$ chmod u+x dir.look
$ _
```

Now the three-line shell script is ready to use. Just move to a directory with cd and type dir.look. The result will look something like this:

```
$ cd ../admin
$ dir.look
Wed Oct 19 11:03:52 PST 1990
```

```
/usr/larry/admin
total 10
drwx--x---  2  paul       258  Jul 18  15:42  answers
-rwxr-x---  1  paul        92  Feb 20  09:14  bates.file
drwx--x---  1  paul       126  Nov 31  08:57  call_FILES
-rw-r-----  3  paul       415  Aug  3  13:09  ddd-125
-rw-r-----  1  paul       361  May 11  10:38  zero+one
$ _
```

In this example, the three commands are all very simple, and
the shell script doesn't really save a lot of time. But you can probably begin to see the potential of a shell script. Suppose you have
commands that are very long and complex. If you store them in a
shell script, you won't have to type them every time you need to
use them.

58 *Adding Another Function*

Let's make the previous shell script more versatile by including
the cd command with the three other commands. This presents a
problem because you want to be able to use this script in any
directory. If you include a directory name in the script, then you
can use the script only for that one directory—not a very useful
script!

The solution is to use a variable name in the script. The variables used to identify the arguments on a UNIX command line are
called *positional parameters*. The notation for this type of variable
includes a dollar sign ($) and a number. By convention, $0 identifies the command name, $1 identifies the first argument, $2
identifies the second, and so on. Here is an example:

```
$ ls     -1      ../admin
$0       $1      $2
```

The cd command requires only one argument (the directory
name). So the identification is even simpler, as in the following:

```
$ cd     ../admin
$0       $1
```

Using this type of variable in the previous shell script will let you change to any directory whose name you specify when you execute the script. All you need to do is include the following line at the beginning of the shell script:

```
cd $1
```

Let's create such a script with the cat command and make the file executable with the chmod command:

```
$ cat > new.dir
cd $1
date
pwd
ls -l
Ctrl-D[] [not displayed]
$ chmod u+x new.dir
$ _
```

59

This four-line shell script now includes the cd command. In essence, you have just created a new command called new.dir that accepts as an argument the name of any directory to which you have access. Following is an example that uses this new command:

```
$ pwd
/usr/paul
$ new.dir /usr/larry/admin
Wed Oct 19 11:12:24 PST 1990
/usr/larry/admin
total 10
drwx--x---   2   paul       258   Jul 18   15:42   answers
-rwxr-x---   1   paul        92   Feb 20   09:14   bates.file
drwx--x---   1   paul       126   Nov 31   08:57   call_FILES
-rw-r-----   3   paul       415   Aug  3   13:09   ddd-125
-rw-r-----   1   paul       361   May 11   10:38   zero+one
$ _
```

Making a Procedure Interactive

So far, you've learned how to write a shell script that runs without any interaction with the user. To make your shell script interactive, you need to know about several more elements of shell programming:

A command to display prompts on the screen (echo)

A command to read input from the keyboard (read)

Variables in which to store user input (of the form $*name*)

Let's refine the previous shell script to illustrate how you can make it interactive. But first, you need to know how to use the echo command. In its simplest form, echo merely displays text on the screen, as shown in the following example:

```
$ echo Hello
Hello
$ _
```

60

By including one of two symbols (and surrounding the text with double quotation marks), you can instruct echo either to keep the cursor on the same line as the message or move the cursor to the next line after displaying the message:

\c   Stay on the same line (good for prompts)

\n   Move to the next line (good for messages)

▶ With a prompt, you want to enter the response on the same line immediately following the prompt. With a message, you want to continue with your work on the next line after you've read the message.

Note that you'll use both of these symbols in the interactive version of your shell script. To create this script, called see, type the following:

```
$ cat > see
echo "Directory: \c"
read dir
cd $dir
date
pwd
```

```
ls -l
echo "Welcome to $dir \n"
```

Ctrl-D /{not displayed}

```
$ chmod u+x see
$ _
```

This seven-line shell script includes cd and interactive programming elements. You have just created a new command called
see that prompts the user for the name of a directory and then
uses that name (by storing it in a variable named $dir). Following
is an example of how to use this new command:

```
$ pwd
/usr/paul
$ see
Directory: /usr/larry/admin
Wed Oct 19 11:12:24 PST 1990
/usr/larry/admin
total 10
drwx--x---  2  paul      258  Jul 18  15:42  answers
-rwxr-x---  1  paul       92  Feb 20  09:14  bates.file
drwx--x---  1  paul      126  Nov 31  08:57  call_FILES
-rw-r-----  3  paul      415  Aug  3  13:09  ddd-125
-rw-r-----  1  paul      361  May 11  10:38  zero+one
Welcome to /usr/larry/admin
$ _
```

61

This time, the command prompts you for the name of the
directory. When you enter a name after the Directory: prompt,
the see command uses that name as the argument for the cd command. Then, at the end of the directory listing, another echo
command uses the name again in its Welcome message.

The Initialization Files

DOS executes a special batch file called AUTOEXEC.BAT every time
you boot your computer. UNIX uses an analogous file when it starts
each command processor. In the Bourne shell, this file is called

.profile; the C shell uses a pair of files called .login and
.cshrc. The rest of this chapter primarily discusses the initialization
file for the Bourne shell. For more information about the C
shell, please see Appendix C.

 For the system as a whole, the startup file is called
/etc/rc.

Using the Shell Start-Up File   *profile*

Each time you log into UNIX, the settings in the .profile file are
used to create your working *environment*. (The C shell calls its
start-up file .login and also uses an additional file named
.cshrc, which contains settings unique to the C shell.) Following
is an example of a simple .profile file in which you assign
values to four shell variables:

```
$ cat .profile
HOME=/usr/ray
PATH=/bin:/usr/bin:$HOME/bin
MAIL=/usr/spool/mail/'basename $HOME'
TERM=tv950
export HOME PATH MAIL TERM
$ _
```

 You can use basename with a full pathname to extract
the last directory name in the string. For example,
'basename/usr/ray' means ray.

The four shell variables are summarized in Table 3-1, and described in greater detail in the paragraphs that follow.

Table 3-1. The Basic Shell Variables

Variable	Description
HOME	Home Directory: The name of the directory that becomes your current directory when you log in.
PATH	Command Search Path: A list of the directories in which UNIX will search for commands that you enter.
MAIL	Mail File: The name of the file to which your incoming mail is sent.
TERM	Terminal Type: The type of video display terminal you are using.

Home Directory. The HOME variable provides the name of your login directory. If you execute the cd command without an argument, the value of HOME is displayed by default. In the previous .profile example, the following two commands are equivalent:

```
$ cd     $ cd /usr/ray
```

Note that the HOME variable (preceded by a dollar sign) is referred to in subsequent .profile entries. In each instance, you can substitute for $HOME the value assigned above (/usr/ray, in this example).

Command Search Path. The directories assigned to the PATH variable must be separated by colons (:). In the previous example, the following directories contain command files available to this user:

```
/bin
/usr/bin
/usr/ray/bin
```

Mail File. The file named here holds your incoming electronic mail messages. In the previous example, the file identified is /usr/spool/mail/ray.

Terminal Type. The terminal type assigned here must be named in one of the following, depending on which is used on your system:

63

```
/etc/termcap
/etc/terminfo/*/*
```

Note that /etc/termcap is a single file, but the /etc/terminfo directory contains a collection of files. A terminal type is necessary only if you plan to use programs like the vi editor, which uses the entire screen.

▶ Notice the fifth line in the previous sample .profile file. The export command causes the four environmental variables to be *exported*, which means that these settings apply to every command that you execute.

64 *Changing the Environment from the Command Line*

It is generally best to set environmental variables in your start-up file; however, you also can set any of them from the command line. The procedure for setting these variables in the Bourne shell differs from that used in the C shell. In the Bourne shell, you must first assign the value and then export the value. In the C shell, you can perform both of these steps with a single command, called setenv. The following example changes the terminal type to VT100:

Bourne Shell	C Shell
$ TERM=vt100	% setenv TERM vt100
$ export TERM	% _
$ _	

The setenv command of the C shell is equivalent to the two Bourne shell commands. (For more information about the C shell, refer to Appendix C.)

What You've Learned

This chapter described the three different command processors, or shell programs, that are used in UNIX systems: the Bourne shell, the C shell, and the Korn shell. The Bourne shell is still regarded as AT&T's official shell.

A command line must contain the name of a command; it may also include additional arguments in the following general format:

$ *name* [*options*] [*files*]

After a command has been executed, a process begins.

You can redirect input and output by using the following symbols and command line syntax:

65

$ command < *file*	Redirect input from *file*
$ command > *file*	Redirect output to *file*
$ command >> *file*	Redirect output (and append) to *file*

You can execute a command in the background by typing an ampersand (&) at the end of the command line. You can display a list of active processes with the ps command. To terminate a background process, use the kill command with the process number as an argument.

The shell allows you to create a shell script, which contains a list of UNIX commands to be executed when you enter the name of the script. Merely enter the commands into a file, and make the file executable with the chmod command. You can use variables, together with the echo and read commands, to make the script interactive.

Initialization of your working environment is accomplished through the use of one file for the Bourne shell (.profile) and two files for the C shell (.profile and .cshrc). These files generally assign values to environmental variables, but they can also contain other UNIX commands.

You can also change environmental variables from a command line using two commands for the Bourne shell (assignment and export) or one command for the C shell (setenv).

Chapter 3 Quiz

1. What is the name of the official System V shell program?

   A. The Bourne shell

   B. The Korn shell

   C. The C shell

   D. The Clam shell

2. Which of the following is required on every command line?

   A. At least one command option

   B. At least one filename

   C. A command name

   D. At least one user's name

3. After you enter a command line, what is activated in the host computer's memory?

   A. A command

   B. A process

   C. An activity

   D. A function

4. Which of the following command lines would you use to redirect input from the file named TEST?

   A. *command > TEST*

   B. *command >> TEST*

   C. *command TEST ¦ command*

   D. *command < TEST*

5. Which of the following command lines would you use to redirect output to the file named TEST?

   A. *command > TEST*

   B. *command >> TEST*

   C. *command TEST ¦ command*

   D. *command < TEST*

6. Which of the following command lines would you use to redirect output to the file named TEST and append data to the file?

A. *.command > TEST*

B. *command >> TEST*

C. *command TEST ¦ command*

D. *command TEST ¦ tee TEST*

7. Which of the following command lines would you use to redirect output of a command to a file and also display the output on the screen?

A. *command > file*

B. *command >> file*

C. *command file ¦ command*

D. *command file ¦ tee file*

8. Which command line would you use to run a command in the background?

A. *command **

B. *command &*

C. *command @*

D. *command #*

9. Which command would you use to find out which commands are running in the background?

A. date

B. who

C. ls

D. ps

10. Which command would you use to terminate a background process?

A. stop

B. cease

C. kill

D. desist

11. True or false: It's possible to place a sequence of UNIX commands in a file, make the file executable, and then execute the commands by entering the name of the file on a command line?

12. What is the name of the variable that indicates the first argument on a command line?

A. %first

B. %FIRST

C. %one

D. %1

13. What is the name of the command that you use to display text on the screen?

    A. `display`

    B. `screen`

    C. `echo`

    D. `show`

14. What is the name of the command for accepting text typed by the user?

    A. `accept`

    B. `read`

    C. `input`

    D. `get`

68

15. What is the name of the Bourne shell's start-up file?

    A. `.profile`

    B. `begin`

    C. `sfile`

    D. `start`

## Chapter 4

Some Utility Programs

What You Will Learn

This chapter describes the most commonly used utility programs of the UNIX system. Here is a list of these utilities, along with their functions:

- ▶ Displaying a calendar (cal)
- ▶ Displaying text on the screen (cat)
- ▶ Printing on the printer (lp)
- ▶ Finding files (find)
- ▶ Finding text in a file (grep)
- ▶ Sorting lines in a file (sort)
- ▶ Performing calculations (dc and bc)

Displaying a Calendar   cal

The cal (calendar) command lets you display a calendar for any year from 1 A.D. to 9999 A.D. For example, to display the calendar for 1991, type the following command:

```
$ cal 1991
```

```
                              1991
           Jan                 Feb                    Mar
  S  M Tu  W Th  F  S    S  M Tu  W Th  F  S     S  M Tu  W Th  F  S
        1  2  3  4  5                   1  2                    1  2
  6  7  8  9 10 11 12    3  4  5  6  7  8  9     3  4  5  6  7  8  9
 13 14 15 16 17 18 19   10 11 12 13 14 15 16    10 11 12 13 14 15 16
 20 21 22 23 24 25 26   17 18 19 20 21 22 23    17 18 19 20 21 22 23
 27 28 29 30 31         24 25 26 27 28          24 25 26 27 28 29 30
                                               31

           Apr                 May                    Jun
  S  M Tu  W Th  F  S    S  M Tu  W Th  F  S     S  M Tu  W Th  F  S
     1  2  3  4  5  6             1  2  3  4                       1
  7  8  9 10 11 12 13    5  6  7  8  9 10 11     2  3  4  5  6  7  8
 14 15 16 17 18 19 20   12 13 14 15 16 17 18     9 10 11 12 13 14 15
 21 22 23 24 25 26 27   19 20 21 22 23 24 25    16 17 18 19 20 21 22
 28 29 30               26 27 28 29 30 31       23 24 25 26 27 28 29
                                               30

           Jul                 Aug                    Sep
  S  M Tu  W Th  F  S    S  M Tu  W Th  F  S     S  M Tu  W Th  F  S
     1  2  3  4  5  6             1  2  3        1  2  3  4  5  6  7
  7  8  9 10 11 12 13    4  5  6  7  8  9 10     8  9 10 11 12 13 14
 14 15 16 17 18 19 20   11 12 13 14 15 16 17    15 16 17 18 19 20 21
 21 22 23 24 25 26 27   18 19 20 21 22 23 24    22 23 24 25 26 27 28
 28 29 30 31            25 26 27 28 29 30 31    29 30

           Oct                 Nov                    Dec
  S  M Tu  W Th  F  S    S  M Tu  W Th  F  S     S  M Tu  W Th  F  S
        1  2  3  4  5                   1  2     1  2  3  4  5  6  7
  6  7  8  9 10 11 12    3  4  5  6  7  8  9     8  9 10 11 12 13 14
 13 14 15 16 17 18 19   10 11 12 13 14 15 16    15 16 17 18 19 20 21
 20 21 22 23 24 25 26   17 18 19 20 21 22 23    22 23 24 25 26 27 28
 27 28 29 30 31         24 25 26 27 28 29 30    29 30 31
```

70

You can also display the calendar for a single month: Merely enter a number from 1 to 12 before you type the year. For example, here is the calendar for June 1991:

```
$ cal 6 1991
   June 1991
  S  M Tu  W Th  F  S
                    1
  2  3  4  5  6  7  8
  9 10 11 12 13 14 15
 16 17 18 19 20 21 22
 23 24 25 26 27 28 29
 30
```

Displaying Text on the Screen   cat

Chapter 3 introduced you to the `cat` (concatenate) command. As its name implies, one of the functions of this command is to concatenate (join) files. For example, to concatenate two files `intro.1991` and `sales.1991` into a new file called `report.1991`, you could use the following command (see Figure 4-1):

```
$ cat intro.1991 sales.1991 > report.1991
```

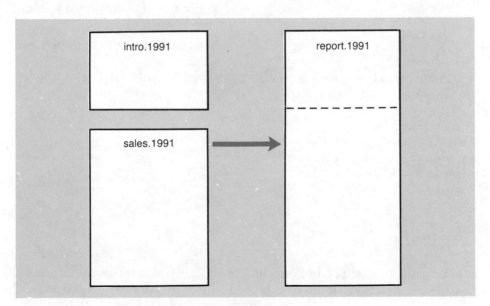

Figure 4-1. Concatenating Two Files

▶ When you use `cat` in this way, be sure the new file (which will hold the combined result) is not one of the original files being concatenated. Otherwise, you will lose text.

Entering Text Manually

If you want to enter the text yourself, rather than use text from existing files, you can omit the names of the source files entirely. Merely type the `cat` command, redirect input to a target file, and type what you want in the file. When you finish, press Ctrl-D to end the file. After you press Ctrl-D, UNIX redisplays the shell prompt. Here is a short example:

`$ cat > sample`	Create a file called `sample`

`This brief statement is`
`an example of creating a`
`small file with cat.`
	Enter the text of the file

	Press Ctrl-D (nothing is displayed)
`$ _`	The shell prompt reappears

72

You can also use `cat` (without redirection) to display the text you have just entered:

```
$ cat sample
This brief statement is
an example of creating
a small file with cat.
$ _
```

Displaying Large Files   *pg*

If you want to display text stored in a large file, you may not want to use `cat` because there will be too much text for your screen. One solution is to use the `pg` command instead. The `pg` (page) command works like `cat`, but, pauses each time a full screen of text has been displayed. Then, you can respond to the prompt at the bottom of the screen (`:`) by pressing Enter. Here is an example:

```
$ pg chapter.5
.
(a screenful of text)
.
: _
```

Some systems also use the `more` command. If this command is available on your system, you have a wider selection of options at the bottom of each page. (It also supplies information about the size of the file by displaying the percentage of the file that you've already read.) Press ? for help. Here is an example:

```
$ more chapter.5
.
{text}
.
--More-- (4%)
```

When the display pauses and the prompt appears, you can choose one of the following options:

- ▶ Press h for help information
- ▶ Press Enter to display one more line
- ▶ Press the Spacebar to display the next screen
- ▶ Begin a search by entering a slash (/) and the text you want to find. (For example, /`select` displays the text that contains the word `select`.)
- ▶ Press Esc to leave the `more` command and return to the shell prompt

73

How the `pg` and `more` commands display discrete screenfuls of text is depicted graphically in Figure 4-2.

 The `more` and `pg` commands, like `vi`, require terminal definitions.

Printing   lp

To print text, you use the `lp` (lineprinter) command. This command, which can route text to any printer in your system, places your request in a *queue* and completes the printing job when the printer you specify is available. If you enter the command in its simplest form, printing is performed on the system's default printer. Here is an example:

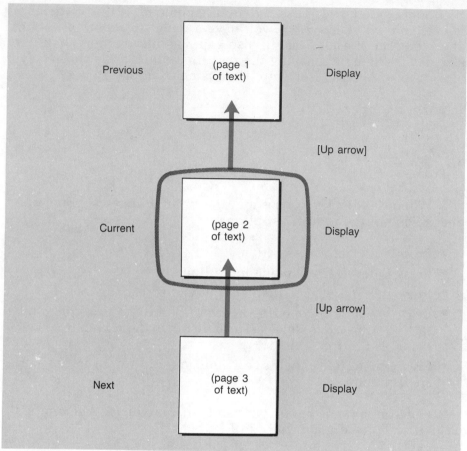

Previous — (page 1 of text) — Display

[Up arrow]

Current — (page 2 of text) — Display

[Up arrow]

Next — (page 3 of text) — Display

Figure 4-2. Paging Text

```
$ lp chapter.5
request id is epson-128 (1 file)
$ _
```

This prints the file chapter.5 on the Epson printer specified as the default for the system.

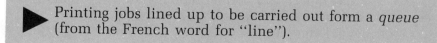

Printing jobs lined up to be carried out form a *queue* (from the French word for "line").

The `lp` command responds to your request with a one-line message that identifies your printing job and tells you how many files have been queued for printing. The identifier includes the name of the printer to which your job will be directed and a sequence number. If necessary, you can cancel the printing job by referring to the identifier, as shown in the following example:

```
$ cancel epson-128
$ _
```

You can also queue several files for printing at the same time, as shown in this example:

```
$ lp chapter.1 chapter.2 chapter.3
request id is epson-136 (3 files)
$ _
```

75

Printing Options

Because all printing jobs must be queued, your request may be delayed while other jobs are being processed. If the printers on a system are very busy, you may have to wait a long time for your printing job to be executed. The `lp` command includes two options that can make the waiting period a little easier to tolerate.

The −m (mail) option tells `lp` to send you a message by electronic mail when your printing job has been completed. The command line would look like this:

```
$ lp -m chapter.5
request id is epson-143 (1 file)
$ _
```

To ensure that the information in your file is backed up, the −c (copy) option tells `lp` to make a copy of your file (or files). Then, if your original files should be misplaced during processing, `lp` can retrieve the backup copy (or copies). You would enter this command:

```
$ lp -c chapter.5
request id is epson-147 (1 file)
$ _
```

Requesting a Specific Printer

In all the examples shown so far, the job has been sent to the default printer (epson). However, if your system uses more than one printer, you always have the option of requesting a specific printer. Furthermore, if your system has many printers and they have been grouped into classes (such as dot matrix printers and laser printers), you can request a particular class. To request either a specific printer or a class of printers, merely include the −d option on the lp command line, as shown in the examples that follow.

To illustrate this feature, let's assume that your system has a printer named nec. (Note that these names will vary from one system to another.) If you want to have a job printed on that particular printer, you can use a command line like the following:

```
$ lp -dnec chapter.6
request id is nec-23 (1 file)
$ _
```

The names for classes of printers also vary greatly. Suppose the printers on your system are grouped into three classes with the following names: matrix (dot matrix printers), daisy (daisy-wheel printers), and laser (laser printers). If you want to be certain that one of your jobs is sent to a laser printer, you can request class laser with a command like this:

```
$ lp -dlaser chapter.7
request id is lw3-52 (1 file)
$ _
```

The message from the printer spooler tells you that your job is queued for lw3 (Apple LaserWriter number 3). Figure 4-3 shows an example of a system that uses nine printers grouped into three classes.

matrix	daisy	laser
mt	nec	lw1
oki	diablo	lw2
epson	qume	lw3

matrix	daisy	laser
mt	nec	lw1
oki	diablo	lw2
epson	gume	lw3

Figure 4-3. An Example of Printer Classes

This example system calls its three classes matrix, daisy, and laser, and lists three printers under each class. Using the –d option described above, you could direct printing to any of these three classes or to any of these nine individual printers.

Displaying the Printing Queue   *lpstat*   77

As noted earlier in this section, printing jobs are queued for all users on the system. To display the print queue after you've requested printing, you can use the lpstat (lineprinter status) command. Here is an example of running this command:

```
$ lpstat
total 28
epson-143       paul       789       May 3 10:09 on epson
epson-147       paul       632       May 3 10:12
nec-23          paul       236       May 3 10:17
lw3-52          paul       189       May 3 10:19
$ _
```

The display is similar to the display for ls –l, with six columns of information. The first column gives the name that lp assigns to your file in directory /usr/spool/lpd, the directory in which the print queue is usually stored.

The lpstat display shows the identifier (printer name and sequence number), your login name, the size of the file in characters, and the date and time of your printing request. The job the system is currently printing is shown on the far right (for example, on epson).

Finding Files   find

The find command lets you search for files and execute a specific action. You can search by filename, type, owner, group, permission, or date of last modification. The action you take can include displaying on the screen, printing, copying, moving, or deleting. The general command line for the find command is shown in Figure 4-4.

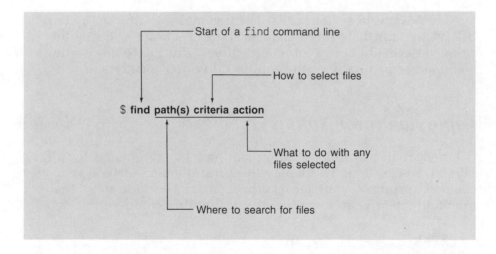

Figure 4-4. The find *Command Line*

The simplest form of the find command merely displays the names of the files you are looking for. It's a good idea to begin every find search with this form of the command. For example, suppose you want to find out how many files in directory /usr are called test.file. To do so, you use the −name option to search by filename and the −print option to display the names on your screen. The command line and output will look something like the following:

```
$ find /usr -name test.file -print
/usr/alfred/control/test.file
/usr/charles/procedures/test.file
/usr/dean/new/test.file
/usr/evelyn/future/test.file
$ _
```

Figure 4-5 gives you a graphical look at the previous command line.

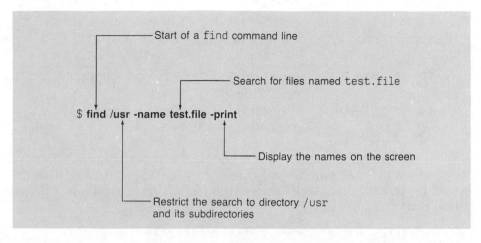

Figure 4-5. A Specific find ***Command Line***

▶ **Note:** In UNIX, the word *print* often doesn't refer to printing on a system printer; instead it refers to displaying text on the screen. When UNIX was being developed in the early 1970s, video display terminals were not yet widely used. TeleType machines were used as terminals, and text was displayed to the user by printing it on rolls of paper. On a video screen, text is *displayed*, not *printed*, but some of the older UNIX terminology still remains.

The first two items on the command line (the name of the command and the pathname) are self-explanatory. However, the third and fourth items (criteria and action) require further discussion.

Search Criteria

You can search for files on the basis of name, type, or numerical information. Some of the search criteria that you can specify include names and types. The following list describes these options:

–name *file*	Search for file(s) named *file*
–type f	Search for an ordinary file
–type d	Search for a directory
–user *name*	Search for files owned by user *name*
–group *name*	Search for files owned by members of group *name*
–newer *file*	Search for files modified more recently than file *file*

The following example uses a few of these search criteria. This command line searches all directories for any ordinary files owned by Evan that have been modified more recently than a file called /usr/paul/entry:

```
$ find / -type f -user evan -newer /usr/paul/entry -print
/usr/evan/test/features
/usr/evan/test/test.mode
/usr/evan/new/memo.201
...
$ _
```

80

Some of the search criteria that you can specify include numbers. The following list describes these options:

	+*n*	Search for files with more than *n* blocks
–size	*n*	Search for files with exactly *n* blocks
	–*n*	Search for files with fewer than *n* blocks
	+*n*	Search for files with more than *n* links
–links	*n*	Search for files with exactly *n* links
	–*n*	Search for files with fewer than *n* links
–ctime	+*n*	Search for files changed more than *n* days ago
–mtime	+*n*	Search for files modified exactly *n* days ago
–atime	–*n*	Search for files accessed fewer than *n* days ago

The following example uses some of these search criteria. This command line searches for all files in /usr that are larger than 10 blocks and that were accessed more than 90 days ago:

> ▶ A *block* is a larger unit of measure in a computer system. In UNIX, a block is typically 512, 1024, or 2048 characters (bytes).

```
$ find /usr -size +10 -atime +90 -print
/usr/alice/memos/memo.302
/usr/carl/news/entry.89
/usr/dale/test/test.493
...
$ _
```

81

Action Statements

The action statements that you can use with find, including -print, are listed below. Two of the statements relate to the cpio command, which is used for copying files to backup devices.

-print	Display the full pathname of each file found
-exec *command*	Execute *command* on each file found (unconditional)
-ok *command*	Execute *command* on each file found (with confirmation)
-depth	Used only before -cpio; copy the files in a directory, and then copy the directory itself
-cpio *device*	Copy each file to *device* in cpio format

> ▶ A directory is a file. If the command can be applied to a directory, it will be.

The −exec and −ok statements require further explanation. If a command uses a filename as an argument, you must type {} \ ; after the name of the command. The empty braces serve as a place-holder for the names of any files to be processed.

The following command line uses the −ok statement:

```
$ find / -name core -atime +7 -ok rm {} \;
< rm ... /usr/paul/plans/core > ? y
< rm ... /usr/quinn/arch/core > ? y
< rm ... /usr/stan/memos/core > ? y
...
$ _
```

This command searches all directories for files called core that haven't been accessed in more than seven days. For each file found, the system prompts you for confirmation. If you answer "yes," the system deletes the file.

82

Searching for Text in a File   grep

Just as find allows you to search for files in the file system, another command—called grep—allows you to search for text in a file or in a group of files. The simplest form of a grep command line includes the name of the command, the text you are looking for, and the name of a file. The output of grep consists of only those lines in the file that contain the text. For example, suppose you want to display all lines in the file sample that contain the word "is." Assuming sample reads as follows:

```
$ cat sample
This brief statement is
an example of creating
a small file with cat.
$ _
```

Then enter a grep command line to conduct the search and display the lines that contain is:

```
$ grep is sample
This brief statement is
$ _
```

Suppose you want to display the name of all files that include the letters ddd. Merely use a pipe between ls and grep to display the matching names, as follows:

```
$ ls -l ¦ grep ddd
-rw-r------   3  paul       415  Aug  3  13:09  ddd-125
-rwx------   5  paul       705  Aug  4  16:15  1-ddd-
txt
$ _
```

In this example, grep doesn't require a filename because ls supplies the text through the pipe. Programs, like grep, that process data are called *filters*.

Searching More Than One File

83

Suppose you have a series of parts lists with names like parts.Bell, parts.Hall, and parts.Smith. For the sake of simplicity, this example includes only these three files, but you could specify many more. Let's begin by looking at the contents of these parts lists.

```
$ cat parts.Bell
Bolt, hex                    00891-00        0.25
Bolt, square                 00784-00        0.18
Nut, hex                     00643-00        0.08
Nut, square                  00675-00        0.06
$ _

$ cat parts.Hall
Plate, rectangular           00632-00        2.15
Bar, square                  00578-00        2.50
Rod, round                   00601-00        2.35
$ _

$ cat parts.Smith
Screw, small                 00329-00        0.02
Washer, round                00274-00        0.03
Washer, round                00407-00        0.05
$ _
```

You can search all of these files with grep. Real parts lists, of course, would be much longer and more complex; however, these small files will clearly show you how to use this important command. Let's use `grep` to answer various questions: For example, does Bell supply bolts?

To determine the answer, check file `parts.Bell` for the word `Bolt`:

```
$ grep Bolt parts.Bell
Bolt, hex                          00891-00           0.25
Bolt, square                       00784-00           0.18
$ _
```

Answer: Yes, Bell supplies bolts.

Let's try another example: Does Hall supply washers? Use the following command to check file `parts.Hall` for the word `Washer`:

```
$ grep Washer parts.Hall
$ _
```

Because the command generates no output, the answer is no.

Does Smith supply small screws? To determine this, check `parts.Smith` for `Screw, small`:

```
$ grep 'Screw, small' parts.Smith
Screw, small                       00329-00           0.02
$ _
```

Answer: Yes, Smith supplies screws.

▶ The quotations marks around `Screw, small` were necessary in this example because you were searching for two words separated by a space.

Let's try one more example: Who supplies washers? To check all three files for the word `Washer`, you can use the following single command:

```
$ grep Washer parts.*
parts.Smith:Washer                 00274-00           0.03
parts.Smith:Washer                 00407-00           0.05
$ _
```

Answer: Smith.

The wildcard symbol * allows you to search all three files (parts.Bell, parts.Hall, and parts.Smith) with a single grep command. Note that when you search more than one file, grep precedes each line of output with the name of the file that contains the line.

Using Regular Expressions

You can use wildcards and other *metacharacters* in searches to match a greater variety of words and expressions. When you use these characters in search strings, you form *regular expressions*. For example, if you want to form an expression that matches either Washer or washer, you could use the following regular expression in your search:

[Ww]asher

85

The following list summarizes the metacharacters available in UNIX:

^	Beginning of line
.	Any single character
[ ]	Specific characters
$	End of line
*	Any number of characters
\	Escape character

▶ If you want to search for one of these characters, precede it with the escape character (\). For example, to search for a dollar sign in a file, you would have to type \$ in the search string.

There are many ways you can use regular expressions to search for text. In the following examples, we'll focus on numbers in the parts.Bell, parts.Hall, and parts.Smith files.

Suppose you want to determine if any items cost exactly $2.50? To do so, you would check all files for the characters

2\.50 (note that to search for a period—which UNIX assumes is a metacharacter—you must precede it with the escape character (\)):

```
$ grep 2\.50 parts.*
parts.Hall: Bar, square            00578-00        2.50
$ _
```

The answer to your query is: Hall's square bar.

Let's try another example: Do any items cost less than $0.10? You can use the following command to check all files for any amounts less than $0.10:

```
$ grep "0\.0[0-9]" parts.*
parts.Bell:Nut, hex            00643-00      0.08
parts.Bell:Nut, square         00675-00      0.06
parts.Smith:Screw, small       00329-00      0.02
parts.Smith:Washer               00274-00      0.03
parts.Smith:Washer               00407-00      0.05
$ _
```

Both of the previous examples illustrate the use of the back-slash to "escape" the decimal point. Without the backslash, UNIX would read the period as a metacharacter. (Note also that the fields were not aligned in the output display.)

Sorting Lines in Files   sort

The sort command allows you to sort (reorder) the lines in a file. If all the text in a file is alphabetic, the lines are arranged in alphabetic order after a sort. Here is an example. Begin with the following file:

```
$ cat flowers
roses
petunias
orchids
daisies
begonias
$ _
```

In the simplest form of a sort command line, you enter only the name of the command and a filename, as shown here:

```
$ sort flowers
begonias
daisies
orchids
petunias
roses
$ _
```

Selecting Fields

You can achieve more sophisticated results with the sort command by choosing a file arranged in columns and then selecting
individual items to sort. For example, take another look at
parts.Hall:

```
$ cat parts.Hall
Plate, rectangular          00632-00        2.15
Bar, square                 00578-00        2.50
Rod, round                  00601-00        2.35
```

From the point of view of the sort command, blank spaces
on a line represent a *field separator*, and therefore each line in
this file contains four *fields*. If you give each field a name, you
can display the file as shown in Figure 4-6.

```
Field 1        Field 2        Field 3        Field 4
Part name      Shape          Part no.       Price

Plate,         rectangular    00632-00       2.15
Bar,           square         00578-00       2.50
Rod,           round          00601-00       2.35
```

Part name	Shape	Part no.	Price
Plate,	rectangular	00632–00	2.15
Bar,	square	00578–00	2.50
Rod,	round	00601–00	2.35
Field 1	**Field 2**	**Field 3**	**Field 4**

Figure 4-6. Fields in a Parts File

Suppose you want to sort the lines by shape. Using notation that is unique to the `sort` command, you would enter the following command:

```
$ sort +1 -2 parts.Hall
Plate, rectangular          00632-00          2.15
Rod, round                  00601-00          2.35
Bar, square                 00578-00          2.50
$ _
```

In this command line, the notation +1 -2 means, "Begin sorting after field 1; stop sorting after field 2." In other words, "Sort only field 2." This is illustrated in Figure 4-7; the vertical lines indicate where sorting begins and ends.

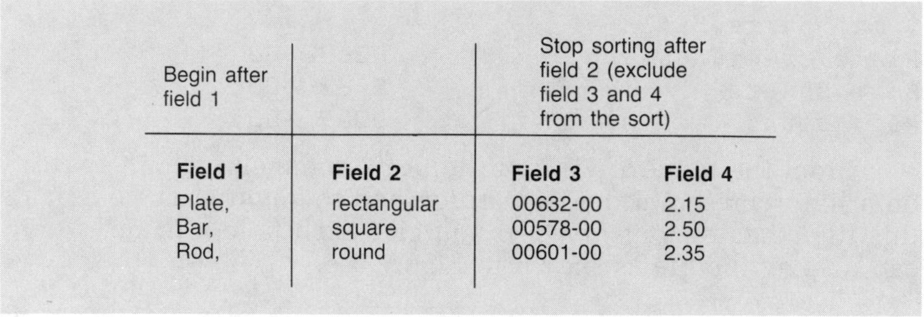

	Begin after field 1		Stop sorting after field 2 (exclude field 3 and 4 from the sort)	
	Field 1	**Field 2**	**Field 3**	**Field 4**
	Plate,	rectangular	00632-00	2.15
	Bar,	square	00578-00	2.50
	Rod,	round	00601-00	2.35

Figure 4-7. Sorting Field 2 Only

Using Sort Options

Next, let's assume you want to sort the lines by part number. Using the field notation from the previous example, you would include the -n (numeric) and -r (reverse order) options, to produce the following command:

```
$ sort -nr +2 -3 parts.Hall
Plate, rectangular          00632-00          2.15
Rod, round                  00601-00          2.35
Bar, square                 00578-00          2.50
$ _
```

In the previous command line, the two options -n and -r are said to be *bundled* (combined after a single minus sign). The notation −nr means, "Sort as numeric information in reverse order. The notation +2 −3 means, "Begin sorting after field 2; stop sorting after field 3." In other words, "Sort only field 3." This is illustrated in Figure 4-8; the vertical lines indicate where sorting begins and ends.

Begin sorting after field 2 (that is, start after field 3)			Stop after field 3
Field 1	**Field 2**	**Field 3**	**Field 4**
Bar,	square	00632-00	2.50
Rod,	round	00601-00	2.35
Plate	rectangular	00578-00	2.15

Figure 4-8. Sorting Field 3 Only

89

The sort command also includes a number of other options, including options for ignoring leading blanks, sorting months of the year, folding uppercase letters onto lowercase, sorting in dictionary order (disregarding case), ignoring non-printing characters, discarding identical lines, merging sorted files, and setting your own field separator. These options are listed in the Quick Reference section at the end of this book; however, a complete discussion of these options is beyond the scope of this chapter.

Sorting More Than One File

You can also sort more than one file at a time. The following command sorts all three parts files by price, highest price first:

```
$ sort -nr +3 parts.*
Bar, square              00578-00        2.50
Rod, round               00601-00        2.35
Plate, rectangular       00632-00        2.15
Bolt, hex                00891-00        0.25
Bolt, square             00784-00        0.18
Nut, hex                 00643-00        0.08
Nut, square              00675-00        0.06
```

continued

```
Washer, round          00407-00        0.05
Washer, round          00274-00        0.03
Screw, small           00329-00        0.02
$ _
```

Sending the Output to a File

Let's conclude this section on sorting by discussing one more important feature—sending the output of a sort to a file (instead of displaying it on the screen). Let's repeat an earlier example in this section with a slight modification that redirects the output. The following procedure sorts the file parts.Hall and sends the recorded output to a file called shape.Hall:

90

```
$ sort +1 -2 parts.Hall > shape.Hall
$ _
```

Display the output file as follows:

```
$ cat shape.Hall
Plate, rectangular     00632-00        2.15
Rod, round             00601-00        2.35
Bar, square            00578-00        2.50
$ _
```

Notice that the sorted output is now in another file, ready to be processed in some other way if necessary.

Performing Calculations

Two UNIX utilities allow you to perform calculations on the screen of your terminal.

Using the Desk Calculator   *dc*

The dc command gives you the convenience of having a simple desk calculator on your screen. The following session illustrates how dc works:

$ dc	Begin a session
6	Enter 6
7	Enter 7
+	Perform addition
p	Display the result
13	
3+p	Add 3 and display the result
16	
9*p	Multiply by 9 and display the result
144	
12/p	Divide by 12 and display the result
12	
9-p	Subtract 9 and display the result
3	
q	End the session (quit)
$ _	

91

Other features of dc include scaling, number bases, subscripts, functions, and logical control. For a complete list of desk calculator commands, see the Quick Reference section at the end of this book.

Using the High-Precision Calculator   *bc*

The bc command brings you a much more sophisticated calculator with unlimited precision, variables, and a range of 0-99 places after the decimal point. The following session illustrates some of the things you can do with bc:

$ bc	Begin a session
17 + 36	Add two numbers
53	
23 - 41	Subtract one number from another
−18	
12 * 13	Multiply two numbers
156	
96 / 12	Divide one number by another
8	
sqrt(64)	Take the square root of a number

```
8
scale = 6                 Request six places after the
                          decimal point
r = sqrt(17)              Assign a value to the variable r
r                         Display the value of r (to six
                          places)
4.123105
define f(x,y) {           Define a function called f
  auto z
z = x - y                 that subtracts y from x
return(z)                 and returns the difference as the
                          value
}                         of function f
a = sqrt(47)              Assign the square root of 47 to
                          variable a
b = sqrt(19)              Assign the square root of 19 to
                          variable b
f(a,b)                    Compute the difference with
                          function f
2.496756
quit                      End the session
$ _
```

92

The bc calculator also allows conversion of numbers from one base to another, arrays, and comments. In addition, the −1 (library) option lets bc use a mathematical library that includes sine (s), arctangent (a), exponential (e), natural logarithm (1), and Bessel (j(n,x)) functions. The following command line invokes the math library:

```
$ bc -l
```

If you often use long functions that are difficult to type repeatedly, you can enter them into a file and then retrieve the file when you begin a session. For example, suppose you store a set of functions in a file called math.bc. When you begin a new session, you can invoke these functions merely by entering the following command line:

```
$ bc math.bc
```

What You've Learned

This chapter introduced you to several utility commands that you will probably use often. You learned how to display a calendar for any year or any month of any year with `cal`.

You learned that you can display text, concatenate files, and even create a file with the `cat` command. The `pg` command is a more convenient method of displaying text in larger files.

The `lp` command lets you print text, either one file at a time or in groups of files, and contains options for notifying you by electronic mail (`-m`) and for making a backup copy (`-c`).

You can search either for files in the file system (`find`) or for text in a file (`grep`). The `find` command lets you manipulate the files you locate with other UNIX commands; the `grep` command merely displays the lines located. Both commands include several options for carrying out extensive searches.

The `sort` command lets you sort the lines in a file using a variety of options, such as selecting fields, sorting numerical entries, and sending the output to a file.

The calculators `dc` and `bc` allow you to perform various computations on your screen. The `dc` calculator is a simple desktop calculator, while the `bc` calculator is a much more sophisticated and precise mathematical tool.

93

Chapter 4 Quiz

Match each command listed on the left with one of the functions described on the right:

1.	`find`	A.	Display a calendar.
2.	`cat`	B.	Combine two files to form a third.
3.	`cal`	C.	Print two files on a system printer.
4.	`bc`	D.	Display all lines in a file that contain a specific word.
5.	`lp`	E.	Display the names of all files in your working directory that you last modified on a specific date.

6. `sort`   F. Arrange all line entries in a file.
7. `grep`   G. Calculate the square root of a number to 20 decimal places.

Write a command line to perform each of the following functions:

8. Display a calendar for October 1562.
9. Create a small file called `test.doc` with the following contents:

   This is a very,
   very small file.

10. Print files `memo.101` and `memo.102` with notification by electronic mail.
11. Locate any files in directory `/usr` owned by user `Penny` that were last accessed more than 30 days ago.
12. Display all lines in files `parts.Bell`, `parts.Hall`, and `parts.Smith` that have part numbers between 00601-00 and 00700-00.
13. Create a new file called `parts.price` that contains one large parts list combined from files `parts.Bell`, `parts.Hall`, and `parts.Smith` sorted by price.
14. Create a new file called `parts.partno` that contains one large parts list combined from files `parts.Bell`, `parts.Hall`, and `parts.Smith` sorted by part number.
15. Compute the value of the square root of 500 to five decimal places.

Chapter 5
Editing with vi

What You Will Learn

This chapter introduces the UNIX text editor known as vi (visual interpreter). You will learn the following:

- ► How to begin and end an editing session
- ► How to move the cursor
- ► How to adjust the screen display
- ► How to insert and delete text
- ► How to move text from one location to another
- ► How to search for text and how to replace text

Beginning and Ending an Editing Session

This section shows you how to start the vi editor, enter text, repeat and undo keystrokes, save your text in a file, and leave the vi editor. It assumes the following two conditions have been met:

Your terminal has been identified to the UNIX system and is ready to perform full-screen editing

You have selected the subdirectory in which you want to work

An Introductory Session

Now you are ready to begin:

1. Start the editor:
   ▶ At the shell prompt, enter the `vi` command, followed by the name of a file:

   `$ vi first.doc`

   ▶ Your screen will soon clear and then display the following:

   ```
   __
   ~

   ~

   ~

   ~

   ~

   ~

   ~

   ~

   ~

   ~

   ~

   ~
   ```

   `'first.doc' [New file]`

2. Select a text-entry mode:
   ▶ Press a (but not Enter) to select the *append* text-entry mode. The a won't appear on the screen.
   ▶ Now, you can begin entering text.

3. Enter your text. For example, type the following paragraph; be sure to press Enter at the end of each line and to insert two spaces after each period:

   ```
   The UNIX text editor is called  vi
   (pronounced by spelling the word).
   The vi editor is actually the visual
   interpreter of the ex editor. When
   you use vi, you will find that the
   two editors become intertwined
   during an editing session.
   ```

   Note that the text appears on the screen as you type it, replacing the tildes on the left side one at a time.

4. Return to the `vi` command mode:

 ▶ To leave text entry mode, press Esc (the Escape key).

 ▶ Again, the screen won't change or display a prompt, but nevertheless you will return to `vi` command mode, from which you can enter editing commands.

5. Write (save) the text to a file and exit `vi`:

 ▶ To write the text to a file named `first.doc`, type `:w` and press Enter.

 ▶ After the `:w` appears at the bottom of the screen, `vi` displays the following message:

 `"first.doc" [New file] 8 lines, 241 characters`

 ▶ To leave `vi` and return to the shell prompt, type `:q` and press Enter; the shell prompt will appear on the screen:

 `$ _`

The previous steps illustrated one complete editing session from beginning to end. You have just used the editor to create a small text file.

Comments on the Session

The preceding steps are typical for any `vi` editing session. You begin by entering the `vi` command from the shell prompt (Step 1). Then you request text-entry mode (Step 2), enter the text (Step 3), and return to command mode (Step 4). Finally, you end the session (Step 5).

 `vi` is actually the visual mode of an editor called `ex`.

The write and quit commands (Step 5) are actually `ex` editor commands. A colon (`:`) always starts `ex` command mode. In Step 5, you entered `ex` command mode twice: first, to write (`:w`) and then, to quit (`:q`). You can either use these commands separately, as you did in Step 5, or you can enter them simultaneously (`:wq`).

 To write text to a file only if it has been modified and then exit, use either `:x` or `ZZ`.

Moving the Cursor and the Screen Display

One of the most basic operations in using an editor is moving the cursor from one location to another. Many of the editing functions of vi work in conjunction with cursor position and cursor motion.

Moving One Position at a Time

If your keyboard has a cursor motion pad with a set of four arrow keys, as shown in Figure 5-1 (left), you can use these to move the cursor. If your keyboard doesn't have these keys, you can use either of two alternative sets of cursor motion keys, as shown in Figure 5-1 (middle and right).

98

▶ On many keyboards, the numeric keypad also serves as a cursor movement pad.

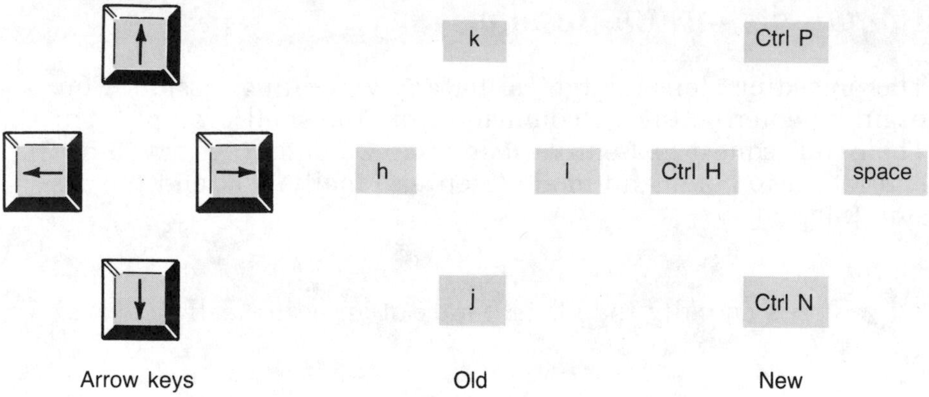

		k		Ctrl P	
←	→	h	l	Ctrl H	space
		j		Ctrl N	

Arrow keys   Old   New

Figure 5-1. Cursor Motion Keys

▶ Remember, case doesn't make any difference when you're using the Ctrl key. Ctrl-P is the same as Ctrl-p.

Remember that these are vi commands. Therefore, you must be in vi command mode to use them. If you aren't sure which mode you're in, press Esc. If you hear a beep, then you are already in command mode.

> Any time you are using vi, you can press Esc to return
> to command mode.

To practice moving the cursor, begin another session and try
the commands you just learned. Then, select the set that you prefer working with. The following command retrieves the file you
created in the previous section:

```
$ vi first.doc
```

After you've experimented with the basic cursor motion keys,
add two more paragraphs to the file (remember to press Enter
between paragraphs and after each line):

```
When you first begin a session with  vi,
you are in vi command mode. To enter
text, press a (or another text-entry
command) to enter text-entry mode.
Once you've entered the desired text,
press Esc to return to vi command mode.

When you're ready to save the text, type
:w and press Enter to write the text
to a file. Then type :q and press Enter
to leave vi and return to the shell prompt.
The colon (:) begins ex command mode, and
the Enter key returns you to vi command
mode.
```

In case you need a reminder, here are the steps for entering
these two paragraphs:

- Move the cursor to the end of the file
- Press a to request append mode
- Press Enter to insert a blank line; then begin typing the text
- After you type the last line, press Esc to return to vi
  command mode
- Type :w and press Enter to write the text to the file
  first.doc (but don't leave vi yet)

After you complete these steps, the editor displays the following message at the bottom of the screen:

99

```
'first.doc' 23 lines, 732 characters
```

Repeating and Undoing Keystrokes

Before we continue discussing cursor motion commands, try the following short exercise, which shows you how to repeat and undo keystrokes. Here are the steps:

1. Enter two lines of text:
    ▶ With the cursor still positioned at the bottom of the file, press Enter and type two more lines of text:

    ```
    These two lines show what you  can
    do with the repeat and undo keys.
    ```

    Then press Esc.
    ▶ The lower part of the screen should look as follows:

    ```
    The colon (:) begins ex command mode, and
    the Enter key returns you to vi command
    mode.

    These two lines show what you can
    do with the repeat and undo keys.


    _
    ~

    ~
    ```

2. Repeat your keystrokes:
    ▶ To repeat these two lines, press the period (.) key (but not Enter).
    ▶ The screen now looks like this:

    ```
    The colon (:) begins ex command  mode, and
    the Enter key returns you to vi command
    mode.

    These two lines show what you can
    do with the repeat and undo keys.

    These two lines show what you can
    do with the repeat and undo keys.


    _
    ~

    ~
    ```

3. Undo the keystrokes:

   ▶ To undo the repeat command (.) of Step 2, press u (but not Enter).

   ▶ The copy of the paragraph will disappear, and the screen will look like this again:

```
The colon (:) begins ex command  mode, and
the Enter key returns you to vi command
mode.


These two lines show what you can
do with the repeat and undo keys.


_
~
```

   ▶ To restore the copy, press u again.

   ▶ To undo the copy again, press u once more.

4. Abandon the extra two lines:

   ▶ To leave vi without saving the extra lines, type :q! (with an exclamation point) and press Enter.

101

▶ The q command requires you to save your text. The q! command allows you to abandon your text.

   ▶ The shell prompt returns to the screen:

```
$ _
```

The repeat command (Step 2) allows you to duplicate a sequence of keystrokes. The undo command (Step 3), which is usually used to undo a deletion, lets you reverse the previous change to your text. Note that when you use the undo command more than once, it reverses itself. These two commands are introduced here because they are so handy in everyday editing.

Moving to the End of the Line

The keys that move the cursor to the beginning of the current line (^) or to the end of the line ($) are the same two characters that are used throughout UNIX in searching for text. You can try these keys now, as shown in Figure 5-2.

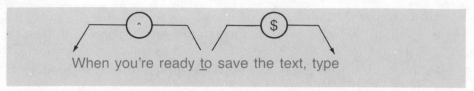

Figure 5-2. Cursor Motion to End of Line

Practice using these keys a few times before you continue with the next section.

Moving a Word at a Time

Now let's examine the commands that move the cursor a word at a time. These commands are illustrated in Figure 5-3.

102

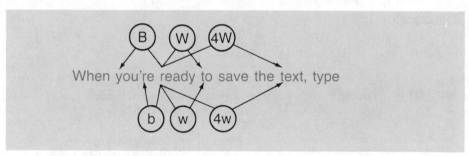

Figure 5-3. Cursor Motion by Word

Use b or B to move one word back; use w or W to move one word forward. The b and B (as well as the w and W) commands are equivalent except that the capitalized versions ignore punctuation, such as apostrophes ('). You can also use a multiplier, such as the 4 in 4w, to move a specific number of words at one time.

Moving a Sentence at a Time

You can use left and right parentheses in vi command mode to move the cursor a sentence at a time. The left parenthesis moves back to the beginning of the current sentence; the right parenthesis moves forward to the beginning of the next sentence, as shown in Figure 5-4.

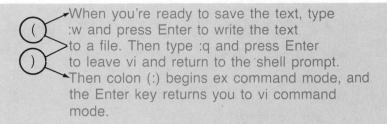

When you're ready to save the text, type
:w and press Enter to write the text
to a file. Then type :q and press Enter
to leave vi and return to the shell prompt.
Then colon (:) begins ex command mode, and
the Enter key returns you to vi command
mode.

Figure 5-4. Cursor Motion by Sentence

▶ If the cursor is already at the beginning of a sentence, the
(command moves the cursor to the beginning of the previous sentence.

Moving a Paragraph at a Time

103

The left and right braces ({ }) function like the left and right
parentheses in vi command mode, but they move the cursor a
paragraph at a time instead of a sentence at a time. The left brace
moves back to the beginning of the current paragraph; the right
brace moves forward to the beginning of the next paragraph, as
shown in Figure 5-5. (The beginning of a paragraph is usually the
blank line that precedes it.)

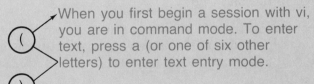

When you first begin a session with vi,
you are in command mode. To enter
text, press a (or one of six other
letters) to enter text entry mode.

Once you've entered the desired text,
press Esc to return to vi command mode.

When you're ready to save the text, type
:w and press Enter to write the text
to a file. Then type :q and press Enter
to leave vi and return to the shell prompt.
The colon (:) begins ex command mode, and
the Enter key returns you to vi command
mode.

Figure 5-5. Cursor Motion by Paragraph

You can use multipliers with the (,), {, and } commands.

Moving Around the Screen

Three capital letters (H, M, and L) allow you to move to one of three locations on the current screen display:

H (high)   Top of screen
M (middle)   Middle of screen
L (low)   Bottom of screen

Practice using these commands now.

104

Moving to a Specific Line Number

Another capital letter, G ("Go to ..."), lets you move the cursor to any line of text, even if that line is not currently displayed on the screen. Merely type a line number in front of the G command, as shown in the following examples:

3G   Move to line 3
7G   Move to line 7
G   Move to the last line

A related command (Ctrl-G) displays the line number at which the cursor is located. Whenever you press Ctrl-G, a message such as the following appears on the screen:

```
'first.doc' [Modified] line 12 of 23 --52%--
```

Now is a good time to practice all these different commands.

Adjusting the Screen Display

This section describes different ways you can adjust the screen display, such as paging, scrolling, repositioning the current line, and clearing system messages.

Paging

Paging is displaying an entirely new screenful of text. The `vi` editor has one command for paging back (Ctrl-B) and one command for paging forward (Ctrl-F), as shown in Figure 5-6:

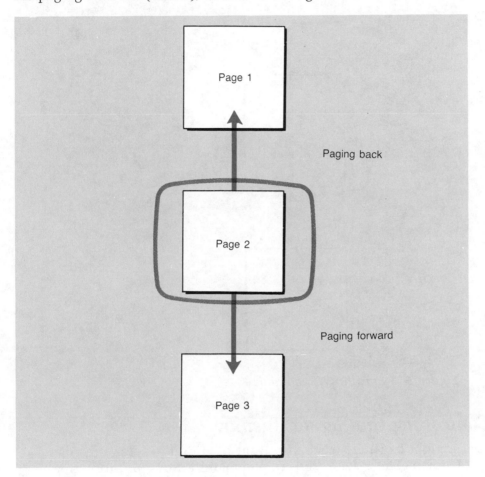

Figure 5-6. Paging Commands

Scrolling

Scrolling, which is similar to paging, is moving the display half a screen at a time. `vi` provides one command for scrolling up (Ctrl-U) and one for scrolling down (Ctrl-D), as shown in Figure 5-7:

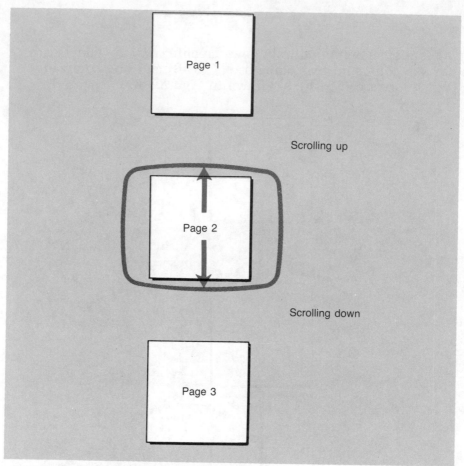

Figure 5-7. Scrolling Commands

Controlling the Screen Display

There might be times when you want to slide the screen display up or down. The z (zero screen) command allows you to perform these operations. By pressing a key after the z command, you can control the placement of the current line on the screen:

z Enter	Place the current line at the top of the screen
z .	Place the current line in the middle of the screen
z –	Place the current line at the bottom of the screen

► Unlike most UNIX commands, which are mnemonically related to their actions (u for "up," b for "back," and so on) the names of these keys are completely arbitrary and meaningless. There is no easy way to remember these three commands.

The commands described in this subsection are illustrated in Figure 5-8.

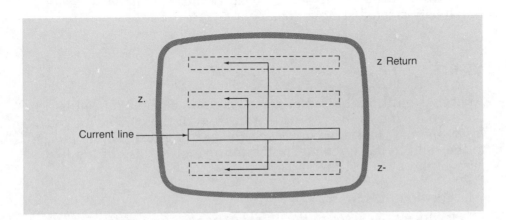

107

Figure 5-8. The Zero Screen Command

Clearing System Messages

Sometimes the system writes messages on your screen while you are working. At other times, vi itself might write extraneous characters on the screen. In either case, you can use the following command to clear messages from your screen and redisplay any lines that might have been overwritten:

  Ctrl-L   Clear messages from your screen

Entering New Text

After you've created a file, you often have to return to the file and add new text to it. vi provides several commands through which you can add the new text, depending on where the new text will be placed in relation to the existing text:

If you want the new text to go in front of the existing text, you can *insert* the new text

If you want the new text to follow the existing text, you can *append* the new text

If you want the new text to be placed on a new line above or below the existing text, you can *open* a new line

In this section, you will try each of these commands in the previously-created sample document `first.doc`.

Inserting Text   *i*

After you position the cursor somewhere on a line, you can use the `i` command to insert new text in front of the cursor. As you insert the new text, the cursor and the existing text will be pushed to the right to make room. Try the following exercise in the first paragraph of `first.doc`.

1. Position the cursor:
   ▶ Move the cursor to the `i` in <u>i</u>ntertwined on line 6:
   ```
   The UNIX text editor is called vi
   (pronounced by spelling the word).
   The vi editor is actually the visual
   interpreter of the ex editor. When
   you use vi, you will find that the
   two editors become intertwined
   during an editing session.
   ```
   ▶ Be sure you are in `vi` command mode.
2. Insert a word in front of <u>i</u>ntertwined:
   ▶ Press `i` to request insertion.
   ▶ Type `completely` (with a space following) and press Esc to return to `vi` command mode.

If you want to insert text at the beginning of the current line, you can either move the cursor and use `i` or you can leave the cursor where it is and use `I` (capitalized). Repeat the preceding Steps 1 and 2, but use the `I` command to insert `fifty-` at the beginning of line 6 (that is, change `two` to `fifty-two`). After you've made this change, the paragraph should look like this:

```
The UNIX text editor is called vi
(pronounced by spelling the word).
The vi editor is actually the visual
interpreter of the ex editor. When
you use vi, you will find that the
fifty-two editors become completely intertwined
during an editing session.
```

Appending Text   *a*

You used the a command in the first session of this chapter. You can use a any time you want to append new text after existing text. The new text will be inserted after the current cursor position; the cursor will remain in its present location, while existing text after the new text will be pushed to the right. Let's use this command in the first paragraph of `first.doc`.

109

1. Position the cursor:
   ▶ Move the cursor to the second l in `will` on line 5:
   ```
   The UNIX text editor is called vi
   (pronounced by spelling the word).
   The vi editor is actually the visual
   interpreter of the ex editor. When
   you use vi, you will find that the
   fifty-two editors become completely intertwined
   during an editing session.
   ```
   ▶ Be sure you are in `vi` command mode.
2. Append a word after `will`:
   ▶ Press a to request append text-entry mode.
   ▶ Type `always` (with a space in front) and press Esc to return to `vi` command mode.

If you want to append text to the end of the current line, you can either move the cursor and use a or you can leave the cursor where it is and use A (capitalized). Repeat the preceding Steps 1 and 2, but use the A command to append `one hundred` to the end of line 5 (that is, change `fifty-two` to `one hundred fifty-two`). After you've made this change, the paragraph should look like this:

```
The UNIX text editor is called vi
(pronounced by spelling the word).
The vi editor is actually the visual
interpreter of the ex editor. When
you use vi, you will always find that the one hundred_
fifty-two editors become completely intertwined during
an editing session.
```

Opening a New Line   o

You have just learned the commands for inserting and appending
text, all of which insert text into the current line. Another pair of
commands allow you to insert text above or below the current
line. We'll begin with the O command, which opens a new line
above the current line. Let's practice using this command in the
first paragraph of first.doc.

110

1. Position the cursor:
   ▶ Move the cursor to the e in editor on line 1:
   ```
   The UNIX text editor is called vi
   (pronounced by spelling the word).
   The vi editor is actually the visual
   interpreter of the ex editor. When
   you use vi, you will always find that
   the one hundred
   fifty-two editors become completely intertwined
   during an editing session.
   ```
   ▶ Be sure you are in vi command mode.
2. Open a line above the first line:
   ▶ Press capital O to open a line above.
   ▶ Type The UNIX Text Editors, press Enter to leave a blank
     line, and press Esc to return to vi command mode.

If you want to open a line *below* the current line, you can use
o (uncapitalized). Repeat the preceding Steps 1 and 2 (without
pressing Enter), but use the o command to open a new line that
says "short for the visual interpreter" below the first line
of the first paragraph. After you've made this change, the display
should look like this:

```
The UNIX Text Editors
```

```
The UNIX text editor is called vi
(short for the visual interpreter)_
(pronounced by spelling the word).
The vi editor is actually the visual
interpreter of the ex editor. When
you use vi, you will always find that the one hundred
fifty-two editors become completely intertwined
during an editing session.
```

This time, use `:wq` (or `:x`) to save the text. A display similar to the following will appear:

```
'first.doc' 26 lines, 831 characters
$ _
```

Figure 5-9 summarizes the commands for entering and exiting the different modes.

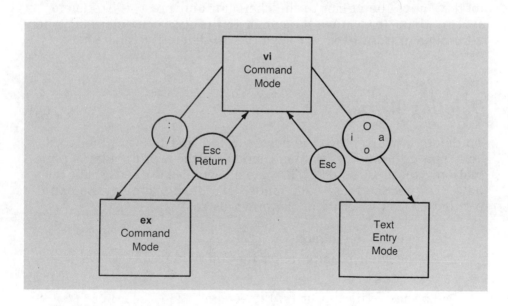

Figure 5-9. Editing Modes

Deleting Text

You probably delete text about as often as you insert new text. The commands for deleting text, like those for moving the cursor, have many variations. You can delete characters, words, lines, sentences, and paragraphs, as well as parts of words, lines, sentences, and paragraphs. The command to delete is d; the letter designators for words, lines, sentences, and paragraphs are the same as those used for cursor motion.

Deleting Characters   *x*

112

The command to delete a character doesn't follow the pattern of the other commands for deleting text. To delete a single character, merely move the cursor to the character and press x. To delete several characters, move the cursor to the first character and type a number in front of x. For example, to delete five characters, use 5x.

Deleting Words   *dw*

To delete a word, move the cursor to the first letter of the word and type dw from vi command mode. (If the word contains punctuation, you must use dW.) To delete several words, use *n*dw (or *n*dW). To practice these commands, let's delete some of the extra words that you inserted in the previous section.

1. Retrieve the document:
   ▶ At the shell prompt, enter the following:
   ```
   $ vi first.doc
   ```
   ▶ The text will appear on the screen.
2. Move the cursor into position:
   ▶ Move the cursor to the first f in fifty-two:
   ```
   The UNIX Text Editors

   The UNIX text editor is called vi
   (short for the visual interpreter)
   (pronounced by spelling the word).
   ```

```
The vi editor is actually the visual
interpreter of the ex editor. When
you use vi, you will always find that the one hundred
fifty-two editors become completely intertwined
during an editing session.
```

▶ Be sure you are in vi command mode.

3. Delete one word:

▶ Type dw to delete fifty-.

▶ Advance the cursor to the c in completely on the same line, and delete it with dw.

▶ Use the same method to delete always on the previous line.

4. Delete several words:

▶ Move the cursor to the o in one hundred.

▶ Type 2dw to delete one hundred.

▶ After these changes, the display should look like this:

113

```
The UNIX Text Editors

The UNIX text editor is called vi
(short for the visual interpreter)
(pronounced by spelling the word).
The vi editor is actually the visual
interpreter of the ex editor. When
you use vi, you will find that the _
two editors become intertwined
during an editing session.
```

Deleting Lines   *dd*

To delete one line, move the cursor to any position in the line and press dd. To delete more than one line, precede the command with a number (*n*dd). Here are some examples:

1. Move the cursor into position:

▶ Move the cursor to the v in visual, which is about the middle of the second line of the paragraph:

```
The UNIX Text Editors
```

```
The UNIX text editor is called vi
(short for the visual interpreter)
(pronounced by spelling the word).
The vi editor is actually the visual
interpreter of the ex editor. When
you use vi, you will find that the
two editors become intertwined
during an editing session.
```
▶ Be sure you are in `vi` command mode.

2. Delete one line:
   ▶ Type `dd` to delete the entire line.
   ▶ The line will vanish, and the cursor will end up on the next line.

3. Delete several lines:
   ▶ Type `3dd` to delete the next three lines.
   ▶ Then, press `u` to restore these lines.
   ▶ After these changes, the display should look like this:

```
The UNIX Text Editors

The UNIX text editor is called vi
(pronounced by spelling the word).
The vi editor is actually the visual
interpreter of the ex editor. When
you use vi, you will find that the
two editors become intertwined
during an editing session.
```

You can also delete text from the cursor to either the beginning of a line (`d^`) or the end of the line (`d$`).

Deleting Sentences   *d)*

For deleting a sentence, we'll move to the second paragraph. To delete a sentence, move the cursor to the beginning of the sentence and press `d )`. Here's an example:

1. Move the cursor into position:
   ▶ Move the cursor to the `T` in `To enter` on the second line:
```
When you first begin a session with vi,
you are in vi command mode. To enter
```

text, press a (or one of six other
letters) to enter text-entry mode.
Once you've entered the desired text,
press Esc to return to vi command mode.

▶ Be sure you are in vi command mode.

2. Delete a sentence:

   ▶ Press d) to delete the second sentence.

   ▶ Press u to restore the sentence.

3. Delete two sentences:

   ▶ Press 2d) to delete the second and third sentences.

   ▶ Press u to restore the sentences.

Because you restored the deleted text in each instance, the display will be unchanged at this point. To delete part of a sentence, move the cursor to the appropriate location in the sentence and press one of the following:

115

d(	Delete to the beginning of the sentence
d)	Delete to the end of the sentence

Deleting Paragraphs   *d}*

For deleting a paragraph, we'll remain in the second paragraph. To delete a paragraph, move the cursor to the beginning of the paragraph and press d}. Here's an example:

1. Move the cursor into position:

   ▶ Move the cursor to the blank line above When you on the first line.

   ‾
   When you first begin a session with vi,
   you are in vi command mode. To enter
   text, press a (or one of six other
   letters) to enter text entry mode.
   Once you've entered the desired text,
   press Esc to return to vi command mode.

   ▶ Be sure you are in vi command mode.

2. Delete a paragraph:

   ▶ Press d} to delete the second paragraph.

▶ After examining the display, press u to restore the paragraph.

3. Delete two paragraphs:

▶ Press 2d} to delete the second and third paragraphs.

▶ Press u to restore the paragraphs.

Because you restored the deleted text in each instance, the display will be unchanged at this point. To delete part of a paragraph, move the cursor to the appropriate position in the paragraph and press one of the following:

d{   Delete to the beginning of the paragraph

d}   Delete to the end of the paragraph

116

Moving Text

Moving text is similar to deleting text. The key concept is that deleted text isn't actually deleted: it's merely placed in temporary storage. To move text from location A to location B, simply follow these four general steps:

▶ Move the cursor to location A
▶ Delete the text with one of the delete commands you just learned in the previous section
▶ Move the cursor to location B
▶ Insert the text with a "put" command, which you will learn about in this section

Because we have already discussed deletion of characters, words, lines, sentences, and paragraphs in some detail, we won't repeat those instructions in this section. Instead, we'll concentrate on moving sentences and merely summarize the rest.

Moving Sentences   *d) and p*

To demonstrate the process of moving text, let's select a sentence in the second paragraph and move it to another location. The following exercise expands on the four general steps outlined previously:

1. Move the cursor to the current location:

   ▶ Move the cursor to the T in To enter on the second line of the second paragraph:

   ```
   When you first begin a session with vi,
   you are in vi command mode. To enter
   text, press a (or one of six other
   letters) to enter text entry mode.
   Once you've entered the desired text,
   press Esc to return to vi command mode.
   ```

   ▶ Be sure you are in vi command mode.

2. Delete a sentence from its current location:

   ▶ Press d) to delete the second sentence.

   ▶ The paragraph should look like this:

   ```
   When you first begin a session with vi,
   you are in vi command mode.
   @
   @
   Once you've entered the desired text,
   press Esc to return to vi command mode.
   ```

3. Move the cursor to the target location:

   ▶ Move the cursor to the T in Then on the third line of the third paragraph:

   ▶ The paragraph should now look like this:

   ```
   When you're ready to save the text, type
   :w and press Enter to write the text
   to a file. Then type :q and press Enter
   to leave vi and return to the shell prompt.
   The colon (:) begins ex command mode, and
   the Enter key returns you to vi command
   mode.
   ```

4. Insert ("put") the sentence at the new location:

   ▶ With the cursor on the T, press uppercase P to insert the sentence at this location.

   ▶ The screen display should now look like this:

117

```
When you're ready to save the text, type
:w and press Enter to write the text
to a file. To enter
text, press a (or one of six other
letters) to enter text entry mode. Then type :q and ...
to leave ·vi and return to the shell prompt.
The colon (:) begins ex command mode, and
the Enter key returns you to vi command
mode.
```

You have now moved a sentence from one location to another. Repeat the preceding Steps 1 through 4 to move the sentence back to its original location. (When you are ready to restore the sentence, press lowercase p in Step 4 rather than uppercase P.) As you can see from this example, successfully moving text depends on getting the cursor in the proper position and using the right "put" command. You can use either of the following two "put" commands:

118

P Insert the text in front of the cursor (or above the current line)

p Append the text after the cursor (or below the current line)

Moving Other Units of Text

You can transpose two adjacent characters by placing the cursor on the first one and pressing xp. For example, suppose you typed hte instead of the. Merely move the cursor to the h and press xp. The x command deletes the h, and the p command puts the deleted character after the cursor (which now is located under the t).

You can move words from one location to another by deleting them from their original location, with commands such as dw, 5dw, 5dW, and then inserting them at the target location with P or p. Delete lines with commands such as dd, 3dd, d^, d$. Delete paragraphs with d{}, d}, d4}, and so on.

 You can use either d5w or 5dw to delete five words. You have this choice for most vi commands.

Finding and Replacing Text

This section demonstrates the `vi` commands that let you find and replace text. The commands are quite straightforward, so you should be able to learn them quickly.

Searching for Text

To search for text from the current location toward the end of the file, merely type a slash (/), followed by the text, and press Enter. The cursor will move to the first occurrence of the text. If you want to search for the next occurrence, press n (next). Here is an example of a simple search:

1. Move the cursor into position:
   - ▶ If you have just opened the file, the cursor will automatically be on the first line.
   - ▶ If you've been working with the file, move the cursor to the first line with the `1G` command.
2. Begin the search for a word:
   - ▶ Type `/you` and press Enter.
   - ▶ The cursor will move to the y in the first you in line 7:

   ```
   The UNIX Text Editors

   The UNIX text editor is called vi
   (pronounced by spelling the word).
   The vi editor is actually the visual
   interpreter of the ex editor. When
   you use vi, you will find that the
   two editors become intertwined
   during an editing session.
   ```
3. Continue the search:
   - ▶ Press n (next) to continue the search.
   - ▶ The cursor will move to the y in the second you in line 7:

   ```
   The UNIX Text Editors

   The UNIX text editor is called vi
   (pronounced by spelling the word).
   The vi editor is actually the visual
   ```

interpreter of the ex editor. When
you use vi, you will find that the
two editors become intertwined
during an editing session.

4. Continue the search again:

▶ Press n again.

▶ Press n six more times to continue the search.

The cursor always moves to the next occurrence of you in this document. To reverse the direction of the search, press N (uppercase) rather than n. If you don't want the cursor to stop at words such as you're, your, youth, and so on, type a space after the u when you begin the search.

To search in the other direction (toward the beginning of the file), initiate the search with a question mark (?) rather than a slash (/).

120

Replacing Text

One of the most useful features of a text-editing program like vi is the ability to search for each instance of a word or expression and replace it with another. This feature allows you to correct multiple spelling errors or change terminology in a file.

The s (substitute) command begins with a colon (:), which signals the change to ex command mode. Follow the colon with the beginning and ending line numbers (separated by a comma) you want to search, the s command, the text you are searching for, and then the text you want to substitute. The following breakdown explains the command in general terms:

*:start,stops/s_string/r_string/*g

in which

:	indicates that this is an ex command
start	is the starting line number of the search
stop	is the ending line number of the search
s	is the substitute command
s_string	is the search string (the text you are looking for)

r_string   is the replacement string (the text to be substituted for the search string)

g   (global) indicates that all occurrences of the search string on a given line are to be replaced, not just the first occurrence

The following example changes each occurrence of vi to vee-eye:

1. Change vi to vee-eye throughout the file:
   ▶ Type the following command:
   `:1,$s/vi/vee-eye/g`
   ▶ Press Enter to make the substitutions.
2. Change vee-eye back to vi again:
   ▶ Type the following command:
   `:1,$s/vee-eye/vi/g`
   ▶ Press Enter to make the substitutions.

121

You can restrict the search by selecting specific starting and ending line numbers. A "line number" can be a number, a search string, or a symbol such as . (current line) and $ (last line). Here are a few examples:

3,.   From line 3 to the current line

.,/step/   From the current line to the first line that contains the word step

.-5,$ From five lines above the current line to the end of the file

What You've Learned

In this chapter, you learned how to begin and end a vi editing session. The session begins in vi command mode. To enter text, you must initiate text-entry mode (using a or one of five other commands), type the text, and then return to vi command mode (press Esc). To write the text to a file, use the :w command; to leave vi and return to the shell prompt, use the :q command.

To move the cursor, you can use one of three sets of keys (or key combinations) to move one position at a time:

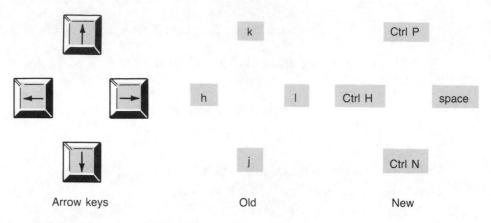

Figure 5-10. Cursor Motion Keys

Other keys that you can use to move the cursor are as follows:

^	Beginning of line
$	End of line
B	Previous word
b	Previous word
(	Previous sentence
{	Previous paragraph
W	Next word
w	Next word
)	Next sentence
}	Next paragraph
H	Top of screen (high)
M	Middle of screen (middle)
L	Bottom of screen (low)
*n*G	Line number *n*
Ctrl-G	Line number?

Keys that alter the screen display are as follows:

`Ctrl-B`	Page back
`Ctrl-F`	Page forward
`Ctrl-U`	Scroll up
`Ctrl-D`	Scroll down
`z Enter`	Current line to top of screen
`z .`	Current line to middle of screen
`z -`	Current line to bottom of screen
`Ctrl-L`	Clear system messages

The six commands for entering text are the following:

`i`	Insert in front of the cursor
`I`	Insert at beginning of the current line
`a`	Append after the cursor
`A`	Append at end of the current line
`o`	Open a line below the current line
`O`	Open a line above the current line

123

Following are the commands for deleting text:

`x`	Character
`dW`	Word
`dw`	Word
`dd`	Line
`d^`	Beginning of line
`d$`	End of line
`d(`	Beginning of sentence
`d)`	End of sentence
`d{`	Beginning of paragraph
`d}`	End of paragraph

To move text from one location to another, delete the text at the original location using one of the commands listed above; then, move to the target location and use one of the following commands:

P Insert the text in front of the cursor (or above the current line)

p Append the text after the cursor (or below the current line)

To conduct a search, type / (or ?), type the search string, and then press Enter. Type n (or N) to continue the search. To replace text, type a command using the form:

`:start,stops/s string/r string/g`

Chapter 5 Quiz

Match each command listed at the left with one of the functions described at the right:

1. }	A.	Move cursor to beginning of line
2. (	B.	Move cursor to end of line
3. ^	C.	Move cursor to previous word
4. H	D.	Move cursor to next word
5. 18G	E.	Move cursor to previous sentence
6. w	F.	Move cursor to next sentence
7. $	G.	Move cursor to previous paragraph
8. M	H.	Move cursor to next paragraph
9. b	I.	Move cursor to top of screen
10. {	J.	Move cursor to middle of screen
11. L	K.	Move cursor to bottom of screen
12.)	L.	Move cursor to line 18

Match each command listed at the left with one of the functions described at the right:

13. Ctrl–D	A.	Page back
14. Ctrl–L	B.	Page forward
15. z .	C.	Scroll up
16. Ctrl–B	D.	Scroll down
17. Ctrl–U	E.	Move current line to middle of screen
18. Ctrl–F	F.	Clear the screen

Match each command listed at the left with one of the functions described at the right:

19.	o	A.	Insert new text at beginning of line
20.	:w	B.	Insert new text in front of cursor
21.	i	C.	Append new text at end of line
22.	a	D.	Append new text after cursor
23.	o	E.	Open new line above current line
24.	I	F.	Open new line below current line
25.	:q	G.	Return to vi command mode
26.	A	H.	Write text to file
27.	:q!	I.	Abandon text without saving
28.	Esc	J.	Leave vi and return to shell prompt

Write a command to accomplish each of the following:

125

29. Delete five lines, including the current line and the next four.
30. Delete text from the current location to the end of the line.
31. Delete text from the current location to the beginning of the sentence.
32. Delete five paragraphs.
33. Delete five characters.
34. Search for the word select.
35. Insert text deleted at another location after the cursor (that is, move the text to the current location).
36. Replace select with choose throughout the current file (every occurrence found).

## Chapter 6

Communicating with Other Users

What You Will Learn

This chapter describes different methods for sending and receiving messages both within your own UNIX system and to other UNIX systems. In this chapter you will learn the following:

- ▶ How to send internal messages with the `write`, `calendar`, `mail`, and `mailx` commands
- ▶ How to send external messages, exchange files, and share resources with the `mail`, `mailx`, `cu`, and `uucp` commands
- ▶ How to access the Usenet bulletin board

Internal Communication

UNIX provides three different facilities for exchanging information between users on the same system: terminal-to-terminal communication, automatic reminder service, and electronic mail. The following sections discuss these features in detail.

Terminal-to-Terminal Communication   *write*

The simplest way to reach another user on your UNIX system is to send a direct terminal-to-terminal message with the `write` command. For example, to reach Janice immediately, you can send her a message like this:

```
$ write janice
Do you still have that report on last-
 month's sales? -o
Ctrl-D
$ _
```

 Note that when you press Ctrl-D, the system does not display a character on your screen.

If Janice is accepting messages, the following appears on her screen immediately:

```
Message from paul (tty05) [Thu Apr 17 09:32:21]...
Do you still have that report on last-
 month's sales? -o
<EOT>
```

If Janice is at her terminal when this message arrives, she can respond with another `write` command back to Paul:

```
$ write paul
Yes.  Do you need it right away? -o
Ctrl-D
$ _
```

To indicate that you have completed a message (or a dialogue), you can establish a simple protocol. You can use -o at the end of each message for "over" and -oo at the conclusion of a dialogue for "over and out."

A message sent with the `write` command appears right on the recipient's screen, often overwriting other displays. If you are engaged in an important task and don't want to be interrupted by `write` messages, you use the `mesg` command to prevent these messages from being displayed on your screen. Merely add the n (no) option, as follows:

```
$ mesg n
$ _
```

After you finish your task, you can accept all messages again by issuing another `mesg` command with the y (yes) option, as follows:

```
$ mesg y
$ _
```

129

Sending Reminders to Yourself   *calendar*

The `calendar` command (not to be confused with the `cal` command) provides you with an electronic reminder service. Since a system utility searches each user's home directory for a file named `calendar` every day (or every other day), all you have to do is create a file with this name and enter your reminders into it. Consider the following example:

```
$ cat calendar
Jun 12    Thursday at 10:00    Department meeting
Jun 16    Monday at 12:00      Deadline for report
Jun 17    Tuesday at 8:00      Monthly PCUG meeting
Jun 20    Friday at 6:00       Farewell party for Steve
$ _
```

The `calendar` command will search this file for you, extract each line that contains either today's or tomorrow's date, and mail any pertinent lines to you. If you prefer, you can also use other formats for the date, such as `June 12` or `6/12`. However, whatever format you choose, each line must contain a date. You don't need to wait for the system to check this file; you can also request your own check by executing the `calendar` command, as follows:

```
$ calendar
Jun 16    Monday at 12:00      Deadline for report
Jun 17    Tuesday at 8:00      Monthly PCUG meeting
$ _
```

Using the Basic Mail Facility   *mail*

You can use the mail command to send electronic mail to any
user on your system. You construct a mail command much the
way you construct a write command, as shown in the following
example:

```
$ mail henry
I hope you have the proposal ready.  We need it by
Wednesday afternoon at 3:00.
Ctrl-D
$ _
```

130

The mail command also allows you to address a group of
users simultaneously, as follows:

```
$ mail anton beverly charles dana
We need to get together some time on Monday to discuss
the forecast for the second quarter. Let me know what
time will be best for you.
Ctrl-D
$ _
```

These messages will not reach their recipients as quickly as a
write message. Each recipient may not become aware of the message until the next time the recipient logs in, as explained in the
following paragraph.

▶ On some systems, you can set a shell variable to allow
immediate notification of incoming mail.

Any time another user sends electronic mail to you, the message will be stored in a file with your login name in directory
/usr/mail. (For example, if your login name is steve, your mail
will be in /usr/mail/steve.) The next time you log in, you will
see the message:

```
You have mail
```

To see what you have received, type the `mail` command without any arguments. The most recent message will appear on the screen, followed by a question mark (?). You can then take action by typing one of the mnemonic codes in Table 6-1. (Note that these often vary from one site to another.)

Table 6-1. `mail` *Options*

Code	Action
`*` (or `?`)	List all the `mail` commands
`p`	Redisplay the current message (print)
`d`	Delete the current message
`m` *user*	Forward the current message to *user*
`s`	Save the current message (with header) in file `mbox`
`s` *file*	Save the current message (with header) in *file*
`w`	Save the current message (without header) in file `mbox`
`w` *file*	Save the current message (without header) in *file*
`Enter`	Display the next message
`!` *command*	Execute *command* without leaving `mail`
`q`	Quit `mail` (retain only unexamined messages in mailbox)
`x`	Exit `mail` (retain all messages in mailbox)

131

Each time you take an action other than exiting `mail` (q or x), the `mail` command displays another message. The following sample session examines several messages:

```
$ mail
From judy Fri Feb 21 10:15:36 1990
We're still working on the sales figures.
Can you wait another week?
? s sales.judy
From will Thu Feb 20 16:08:49 1990
I need the sales figures for the Monday
morning meeting.  Can you help me?
? m judy
From peter Thu Feb 20 13:27:42 1990
Can you play tennis this Saturday morning?
```

```
We're going to play doubles at 10:00.
? q
$ mail peter
Yes! I'll be there at 9:30 to warm up.
Ctrl-D
$ _
```

In this sequence, you saved the first message in a file called
sales.judy. Next, you forwarded the second message to Judy.
Then, you quit mail and returned to the shell prompt, from which
you mailed a response to the third message. Because you used the
q command to leave mail, the three messages you previously
examined will be gone the next time you check your mail.

If you want to reverse the order in which your messages are
displayed, so that the first one received is also the first one displayed, you can use the −r (reverse order) option, as follows:

132

```
$ mail -r
From peter Thu Feb 20 13:27:42 1990
Can you play tennis this Saturday morning?
We're going to play doubles at 10:00.
? _
```

The −f option of mail lets you display mail in a file that you
choose. Ordinarily, your mail is stored in /usr/mail/*name* (in
which *name* is your login name). If you don't specify a name after
the command, UNIX uses the default name mbox. The following
two examples show how to use this option:

$ **mail −f**   Read mail in file
                  /usr/*name*/mbox

$ **mail −f sales**   Read mail in file
                  /usr/*name*/sales

Using the Extended Mail Facility   *mailx*

The mailx command, which is actually the Berkeley mail command, is an enhanced version of mail that contains many more
features. If it is available on your system, you can use mailx
instead of mail. One difference you will notice right away is that
mailx displays a Subject prompt that lets you give your message

a title before you actually type. Here is an example of sending mail with `mailx`:

```
$ mailx anton beverly charles dana
Subject: Meeting on Forecast
We need to get together some time on Monday to discuss
the forecast for the second quarter. Let me know what
time will be best for you.
Ctrl-D
$ _
```

Another enhancement of `mailx` lets you interrupt text entry in the middle of your message, execute a command, and then resume typing your message. For example, suppose you are in the middle of your message and you suddenly remember that you omitted James and Elaine from the list of addressees. You can *escape* from the message with a command such as the following:

133

```
~t james elaine
```

Every escape command begins with a tilde (~) and includes at least one other character (t in the previous example). Some of the other escape commands available in `mailx` are listed in Table 6-2.

Table 6-2. Escape Commands

Command	Action
~?	List all escape commands
~s *subject*	Enter a subject title called *subject*
~t *user(s)*	Add users to the "To" list
~c *user(s)*	Add users to the "Copy" list
~h	Display "To," "Subject," and "Copy" prompts
~r *file*	Read text into your message from another file
~w *file*	Write your message to another file
~v	Use `vi` to edit your message
~p	Display (print) the current message
~f *message(s)*	Read in other messages
~m *message(s)*	Read in other messages (indented to the first tab stop)

(continued)

Table 6-2. *(continued)*

Command	Action
~! *command*	Run a UNIX command and return to `mailx`
~| *command*	Pipe the message through *command* (UNIX command)
~q	Quit `mailx` (save current message in file `dead.letter`)
~x	Exit `mailx` (discard current message)

To find out whether you have received any messages from other users, enter the `mailx` command without any options. The `mailx` command then summarizes the mail you have received by displaying a *header* (a one-line synopsis) for each message. Each header is assigned a sequence number and is labeled with a one-letter code near the left margin:

N   New

R   Read

U   Unread

The `mailx` command also displays the size of the message in lines and characters (for example, 3/96), an optional "subject," a pointer to the current message, and a question mark prompt, as shown in the following example:

```
$ mailx
'/usr/mail/jeff': 5 messages 2 new 3 unread
 U  1 james    Tue Apr 16 09:36    3/96     Goals meeting
 U  2 paul     Tue Apr 16 09:51    4/104    Clock times
 U  3 nancy    Tue Apr 16 11:23    2/72
 N  4 ralph    Tue Apr 16 11:42    5/167    VCR type
>N  5 kelly    Tue Apr 16 12:05    3/89     PTV changes
?
```

At the ? prompt, you can use any of the commands in Table 6-3. The full command names are shown here, but the first letter is all you have to enter. In the following table, *list* is always optional (as indicated by the brackets). By default, it represents the current message. However, you can define *list* so that it becomes a list of messages specified by number, sender, type, or subject.

Table 6-3. `mailx` *Commands*

Command	Action
?	List all commands with explanations
list	List all commands without explanations
headers [*list*]	Display designated headers
z	Display the next page of headers
z –	Display the last page of headers
from [*list*]	Display header(s)
top [*list*]	Display only the first five lines of message(s)
next [*message #*]	Display the next message
type [*list*]	Display message(s) (same as `print`)
preserve [*list*]	Preserve message(s) in `mbox` (same as `hold`)
save [*list*] *file*	Save message(s) (append) to *file*
delete [*list*]	Delete message(s)
undelete [*list*]	Undelete deleted message(s)
edit [*list*]	Edit message(s)
Reply [*list*]	Reply to sender only
reply [*list*]	Reply to sender and to other recipients
cd [*directory*]	Change to *directory* (home if name omitted)
	command	Execute UNIX command and return to `mailx`
quit	Quit (save only unread messages in `mbox`)
exit	Exit (save all messages in `mbox`)

135

The –f option of `mailx`, like its counterpart in `mail`, lets you display mail in a file that you choose. Ordinarily, your mail is stored in /usr/mail/*name* (in which *name* is your login name). If you don't specify a name after the command, UNIX uses the default name mbox. The following two examples show you how to use this option:

$ **mailx –f**	Read mail in file
/usr/*name*/mbox	
$ **mailx –f sales**	Read mail in file
/usr/*name*/sales	

External Communication

UNIX offers several ways to communicate with users on other UNIX systems, including the cu (call up) and uucp (UNIX-to-UNIX copy) commands. The following sections describe these commands in detail.

Calling Another System *cu*

The cu (call up) command allows you to communicate with another UNIX (or non-UNIX) system by dialing a telephone number. With this simple command, you can access any machine with a phone number and a serial port. If you have the proper permissions, you can also communicate with another UNIX system and log into it as if you were a local user. A technician or a programmer could use this command to log into a UNIX system remotely and conduct diagnostic or other tests. The cu command can also be used to test connections when you set up uucp for your UNIX system.

For example, suppose the number for another system is (408) 555-2000, and suppose both systems have been set up to communicate at a rate of 2400 bits per second. Then you could use a command such as the following to call the other system. Assuming that the other system is also a UNIX system and that you have established a login account on that system, you can then proceed to log in, as shown in the following sequence:

```
$ cu -s2400 4085552000

Connected
login: paul
Password:

% _
```

 Specify the data rate (or speed) with the -s option. The telephone number doesn't require an option letter.

For the sake of simplicity, let's assume that the other system presents a C shell prompt. After you're connected, you can execute some commands on your own system and some on the other system. If you remember that the C prompt (%) represents the other system, we can eliminate some of the confusion in the discussion that follows.

If another system—called `gemini`—belongs to your `uucp` network, you may be able to call the system with a simpler command line than in the previous example:

```
$ cu gemini

Connected
login: paul
Password:

gemini% _
```

137

If the serial line or modem on the other system is busy, then you may not get a connection right away, and the sequence will look like this:

```
$ cu gemini

Connect failed: No Device Available

$ _
```

If you use the wrong name, or a name that is not listed in the appropriate `uucp` file (see below), the sequence may look like this:

```
$ cu lemony

Connect failed: Requested device/system name not known.

$ _
```

A certain file contains the names of the systems on the `uucp` network that you can access. Before System V, Release 3, this file was called `/usr/lib/uucp/L.sys`; since System V, Release 3, its name has been changed to `/usr/lib/uucp/Systems`. To display a list of these systems, use the `uuname` command, as follows:

```
$ uuname
gemini
saturn
jupiter
neptune
venus
$ _
```

After you've made a connection and logged in, you can use several commands to interact with that system. For example, to send a file called `report` to the other system (UNIX or non-UNIX), you could use a command such as the following:

```
% ~> report
18 lines/1324 characters
% _
```

138

If both are UNIX systems and if you have the necessary permissions, you can use the following command to send a file:

```
% ~%put report
```

... {system message}

```
% _
```

If both are UNIX systems and if directory permissions give you the authority, you can copy a file from the other system to your working directory. Here is the command:

```
% ~%take sale
```

...{system message}

```
% _
```

To run a command on your own system (as though you weren't connected to another system), precede the command by `~!`. For example, to display today's date, you could use the following command:

```
% ~!date
Tue Mar 3 09:38:12 PST 1990
% _
```

Although you will see the output of date on your screen, the other system will never even be aware that you entered the command.

To run a command on your own system, but send the output to the other system (rather than to your terminal), precede the command with ~$. For example, suppose you would like to send a file to a non-UNIX system. First, make sure the other system is prepared to receive a file; then, enter a command such as the following:

```
% ~$put sales.1990
% _
```

This sends the text to the other system, not to your terminal. After the other system has received the file, you will regain access to that system.

To change directories on your own system, use cd with the prefix ~%, not ~!, as shown here:

139

```
% ~%cd admin
% _
```

After you've finished exchanging files, you can log out and terminate the cu session with the ~. command, as follows:

```
% Ctrl-D
login: ~.
Disconnected
$ _
```

The Bourne shell prompt is from your own system, and it indicates that the cu session is over. In some instances, the ~. command may log you out and disconnect the systems at the same time.

Sometimes it can be useful to keep a record of your communication with another system by capturing the session in a file. You can do this by piping the entire session through the tee command. The following command line illustrates how you could begin the cu session:

```
$ cu -s2400 4085552000 : tee capture.file

Connected
login: paul
Password:

% _
```

Now, proceed through the session as described in this section, exchanging files as desired. After you end the session and return to your own system, you can display the contents of the capture file with a command such as the following:

```
$ pg capture.file

[Remote session]

$ _
```

140

UNIX-to-UNIX Communication   *uucp*

Strictly speaking, uucp (UNIX-to-UNIX copy) is just one UNIX command that is used for copying files. However, in everyday conversation, the term uucp is understood to include a suite of related commands (uucp, uux, and others), along with a network of UNIX systems and an inter-system mail facility. If uucp has been set up on your system, you can send mail to and receive mail from users on other systems, copy files to other systems, and execute commands on other systems.

The uucp network provides UNIX users with something similar to what commercial information services such as *CompuServe* and *The Source* provide personal computer users. One difference is that uucp is included with each UNIX system at no extra charge. For UNIX systems in the same building, uucp offers a means of sharing resources, such as laser printers, plotters, and high-speed tape drives.

After uucp has been set up on your system and on other systems, you can send mail to users on all of those systems as if they were on your own. For the simplest example, let's assume that your system is connected directly to another system called neptune and that you want to send a message to user bill. Then, you could send your message in the following way:

```
$ mail neptune!bill

The volleyball tournament will begin Saturday
afternoon at 1:00 in Green Oaks Park. Can you make it?

Terry
Ctrl-D
$ _
```

On the uucp network, the exclamation mark (!) functions like the slash (/) within your own system's file system. The exclamation mark (sometimes pronounced "bang") separates the name of one system from the name of another and separates the name of the destination system from the name of the user.

After the message has been forwarded to neptune, Bill has been notified, and Bill checks his mail, Bill will see something like the following:

```
From uucp Tue Apr 19 14:06 PDT 1990
>From terry Mon Apr 18 17:23 PDT 1990 remote from jupiter
Status: R

The volleyball tournament will begin Saturday
afternoon at 1:00 in Green Oaks Park. Can you make it?

Terry
```

Now Bill can reply, using a command such as the following:

```
$ mail jupiter!terry
Yes. I'll bring Paula with me.
Ctrl-D
$ _
```

Naturally, sending electronic mail to a user on another system takes even longer (usually at least a day) than to a user on your own system. However, if the other system is very far away, this can still be a fast way to communicate.

Next, suppose the user to whom you want to send a message is on a system that is not directly connected to yours. In that case, you will have to route your message through other systems. For example, Figure 6-1 shows a group of UNIX systems connected in a uucp network.

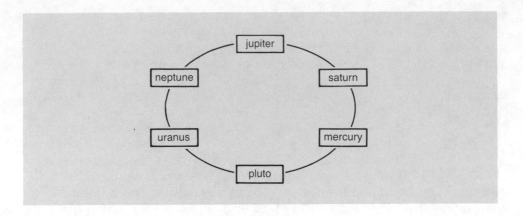

Figure 6-1. A Few UNIX Systems on a Network

Bill can't send mail from his system (neptune) directly to Jeff on system mercury. Instead, he has to route it through jupiter and saturn, as shown in the following example:

```
$ mail jupiter!saturn!mercury!jeff
The volleyball tournament will begin Saturday
afternoon at 1:00 in Green Oaks Park. Can you make it?

Bill
Ctrl-D
$ _
```

People who work on UNIX systems every day and communicate through any kind of public forum often list their uucp addresses instead of their phone numbers for replies. It is not uncommon to see a listing such as the following at the end of a notice on an electronic bulletin board or following an article in a magazine:

```
J. R. Ewing
utvax!dallas!southfork!jre
```

The last three letters in this example represent a login
name.

This listing gives you the routing information you need to
send a message to "J. R. Ewing." If there are several alternate
routes to the destination, these are listed between a pair of braces,
as shown in the following address path:

```
{ucivax,trwb}!ucla-cs!lcc!hxn
```

This address is equivalent to the following two addresses, and
you are free to select either address:

```
ucivax!ucla-cs!lcc!hxn
trwb!ucla-cs!lcc!hxn
```

143

Next, we'll discuss the second main function of the `uucp` network, which is copying files to other systems. In the interest of
system security, one directory (called `/usr/spool/uucppublic`)
has been designated as the place to send and receive files between
systems. Therefore, the procedure for sending a file to someone on
another system requires the following four steps:

- ▶ If necessary, give other users read permission for the file
- ▶ Use the ordinary `cp` command to copy the file from your
  working directory to `/usr/spool/uucppublic`
- ▶ Use `cd` to move to `/usr/spool/uucppublic`
- ▶ Use `uucp` to copy the file to the other system

In the following example, Terry on system `jupiter` sends a
file named `/usr/terry/admin/sales.1990` to Bill on system
`neptune`. (For the sake of simplicity, let's assume that the two
systems are directly connected on the `uucp` network.)

```
$ pwd
/usr/terry/admin
$ chmod o+r sales.1990
$ cp sales.1990 /usr/spool/uucppublic
$ cd /usr/spool/uucppublic
$ uucp sales.1990 neptune!/usr/spool/uucppublic/sales.1990
$ _
```

The last command line can be abbreviated by substituting ~/ for /usr/spool/uucppublic, as follows:

```
$ uucp sales.1990 neptune!~/sales.1990
$ _
```

If you're using the C shell, you must escape each exclamation mark with a backslash (\), as shown on the following command line:

```
$ uucp sales.1990 neptune\!/usr/spool/uucppublic/sales.1990
$ _^
```

 The exclamation mark has another meaning in the C shell.

You can use the -m option of the uucp command to have UNIX mail you a message after the copy has been completed, as shown on this command line (Bourne shell):

```
$ uucp -m sales.1990 neptune!/usr/spool/uucppublic/sales.19
$ _^
```

Once a copy of sales.1990 has been placed in /usr/spool/uucppublic on system neptune, a message to this effect will be mailed to the sender.

The uucp command, like the cp command, supports the use of wildcard characters for selecting files. For example, suppose Terry wants to send three files called sales.1990, costs.1990, and summary.1990. The complete sequence for copying these files will be as follows:

```
$ pwd
/usr/terry/admin
$ cp *.1990 /usr/spool/uucppublic
$ cd /usr/spool/uucppublic
$ uucp *.1990 neptune!~/
$ _
```

The third major function of uucp is that it lets you execute commands on another system with the uux command. Suppose system `neptune` has a laser printer that is being shared by several other systems, including `jupiter`. In that case, a user on `jupiter` can route printing requests to the laser printer by executing a command like the following:

```
$ cat report ¦ uux - neptune!lp
$ _
```

 The minus sign is used to take the name of the file already indicated on the command line.

The `cat` command on system `jupiter` will pipe the file to `uux`, which will then execute the `lp` command on system `jupiter`, which will queue the printing request. The originator will receive a mail message like the following:

145

```
From uucp Thu Mar 17 10:43 PST 1991
>From uucp Thu Mar 17 11:15 PST 1991 remote from neptune
Status: R

uuxqt cmd (lp) status (exit 0, signal 0)
```

Using the Unix Bulletin Board

Several networks, including `uucp`, ARPANET, Berknet, and X.25, provide an environment for an informal bulletin board called Usenet (Users' Network). If Usenet has been set up at your installation, you can participate in the discussions on it. You can read notices that have been posted by other users, and you can post your own notices for others to read.

Newsgroups

Notices are categorized into approximately 250 newsgroups, each of which contains messages concerning a limited special-interest subject. These newsgroups focus on various academic subjects, political issues, and recreational activities. The newsgroups have been placed in a set of seven major categories (see Table 6-4). Note that your installation may have added specialized newsgroups.

Table 6-4. Usenet Categories

Category	Description
comp	Computer science
misc	Miscellaneous
news	Net news and net users
rec	Recreational activities
sci	Natural sciences
soc	Social topics
talk	Discussion topics

146

To find out exactly which newsgroups are found at your site, you can display the contents of /usr/lib/news/newsgroups, using either the pg or more commands, as follows:

```
$ more /usr/lib/news/newsgroups
ca.general          Of general interest to readers in
                    California only
ca.driving          California freeways and backroads
ca.earthquakes      What's shakin' in California
ca.environment      Environmental concerns in California
ca.news             USENET status and usage in California
ca.news.group       Existing or proposed newsgroups for 'ca'
                    distribution
ca.politics         Political topics of interest to California
                    readers only
ca.test             Tests of 'ca' distribution articles
ca.unix             Unix discussion/help
ca.wanted           For Sale/Wanted postings throughout
                    California
junk                Articles that we have no newsgroup for
comp.ai             Artificial intelligence discussions
comp.ai.digest      Artificial Intelligence discussions
                    (Moderated)
comp.ai.edu         Applications of Artificial Intelligence
...                 to Education
$ _
```

Some newsgroups are for specific geographic areas (as in many of groups in the previous listing). There may be a category for your state, using the two-letter postal abbreviation as a prefix. For example, you may find the groups ca.driving, ca.wanted, and so on in California-based systems. Other prefixes include usa (United States), can (Canada), na (North America), and so on.

One of the first things you need to do after you peruse the bulletin board is to select the newsgroups that interest you. (A list of newsgroups is called a *subscription list*, and the act of indicating a preference for a particular newsgroup is referred to as *subscribing* to that newsgroup.) On Usenet, as on most bulletin boards, commercial notices are not welcome.

Reading the Bulletin Board

147

Checking the bulletin board is similar to checking your mail. You request a look at the notices for the day, the first notice appears, and you have a number of options you can select. To read the day's news, you can use one of three commands (`readnews`, `vnews`, or `rn`), depending on what is available at your installation. In this chapter, we'll assume that you are using `readnews`. You can use the following command from the shell prompt:

```
$ readnews
```

If you want to review your current subscription list, you can include the -s option, as follows:

```
$ readnews -s
```

To show only those articles that belong to newsgroups `rec.games.chess` and `rec.pets`, you can use a command line like the following:

```
$ readnews -n rec.games.chess rec.pets
```

The options that are available to you when you are perusing the day's articles are listed in Table 6-5.

Table 6-5. Bulletin Board Options

Option	Action
?	Help
N	Go to the next newsgroup
U	Unsubscribe from the current newsgroup
b	Back up one article in the current newsgroup
−	Return to the previous article
+	Skip the current article
e	Erase the current article
s *file*	Save the current article in *file*
r	Reply to the author of an article
f	Post a follow-up to an article
Del	Delete the rest of an article
x	Exit

148

Writing to the Bulletin Board

If you want to comment about an article that you've read, use the
f option (follow-up) listed in Table 6-5. Then your comment will
automatically be associated with the original article.

If you want to comment about something not previously
referred to in Usenet, use the postnews command in most
instances (or Pnews if your system has rn). Here is how to begin:

```
$ postnews
Is this message in response to some other message? n
Subject: Bird-watching in eastern Missouri
Keywords: birds cardinals

Newsgroups (enter one at a time, end with a blank line):

For a list of newsgroups, type ?
> rec.birds
>

Distribution (default='mo', '?' for help) : mo
```

When the opening prompt asks you whether this is a follow-up, your answer should be no. (If the answer is yes, use the f option of `readnews`, not `postnews`.) If your reply is no, the next prompt asks you for the subject of your article. Enter a name that is as specific as possible.

Next, you will be prompted for pertinent newsgroups. If you aren't sure, type ? to display a list and make your selection. After this, you will be prompted for distribution to other users. Restrict the distribution to the smallest geographic area possible.

Finally, the editor will begin, and you can enter the text of your article. After you've saved your article, you will see a message such as the following:

```
Posting article ...
Article posted successfully.
A copy has been saved in /usr/paul/author_copy
```

You may also leave a signature at the end of each article posted with `postnews` (or `Pnews`). Merely place the desired information in your home directory in a file called `.signature`, and your posting program will automatically insert it for you. Here is an example of such a file:

149

```
$ cat .signature
Paul Fletcher  (213) 555-1212
4243 Wilshire Boulevard
Beverly Hills, CA 90211
ucivax!ucla-cs!projects!paul
```

Setting Up to Use the Bulletin Board

Unless you specify otherwise, Usenet will give you a default subscription list, usually consisting of the "general" newsgroups. To select your own newsgroups, you can enter a customized subscription list in your home directory, using a file named `.newsrc`. (The file must have this name; no other name can be used.)

For example, suppose you want to subscribe to newsgroups `rec.arts.books`, `news.misc`, `comp.unix`, and `ca.general`. Merely create a file called `.newsrc` (or retrieve the file if it already exists), and enter these names on the "options" line. Separate individual names with commas, as illustrated here:

```
$ cat .newsrc
options -n rec.arts.books,news.misc,comp.unix,
ca.general
$ _
```

If your list requires more than one line, begin each subsequent line with a blank space. Note that when you start readnews, the articles are displayed in the order you indicate in .newsrc.

When setting up your subscription list in .newsrc, you can use the "all" option to select all of a set of newsgroups or the ! symbol to exclude all of a set. For example, to include everything related to UNIX, but exclude all talk news, you could set up the "options" line as follows:

```
$ cat .newsrc
options -n comp.unix.all,!talk.all
$ _
```

What You've Learned

This chapter described several different ways you can communicate with other users, either on your own system or on other systems. On your own system, you can send messages directly to other users with the write command, you can set up reminders for yourself with the calendar command, and you can send and receive messages via electronic mail with the mail and mailx commands.

The rest of the facilities discussed in this chapter show you how to communicate with users on other systems. The cu command lets you dial a telephone number and log into a UNIX (or non-UNIX) system. After you're logged in, you can send and receive files in various ways.

The uucp feature (which includes nine UNIX commands and a network of UNIX systems) allows inter-system electronic mail, the exchanging of files, and the remote execution of UNIX commands. Usenet, which operates over several networks, including uucp, offers a bulletin board with articles posted according to the interests of specific newsgroups. You can read articles posted by other users around the world and post your own articles for others to read.

Chapter 6 Quiz

Match each command listed at the left with a function described at the right:

1. mail
   A. Send a message directly from your terminal to another user's terminal (same system)

2. uucp
   B. Prevent messages from being sent by other users to your terminal

3. mesg
   C. Send a reminder to yourself about an appointment

4. mailx
   D. Send a message to another user either on your own system or on another system

5. postnews
   E. Send a message to another user via the extended electronic mail facility

6. write
   F. Call another UNIX system to check out the dial-in number

7. readnews
   G. Send a copy of one of your files to a user on another system

8. cu
   H. Print a copy of one of your files on another system

9. calendar
   I. Read today's articles on the Usenet bulletin board

10. uux
   J. Post an article of your own on the Usenet bulletin board

151

Write a command (or a series of commands) to perform each of the following functions:

11. Send a message, which you have stored in a file called hello, directly to Sean (login name sean).
12. Prevent messages from being sent directly to your terminal.
13. Check on reminders that you have left for yourself.
14. Send a message, which you have already typed and stored in a file called urgent, to Linda, Mike, and Paula (login names linda, mike, and paula) via electronic mail.
15. Check for electronic mail that you've received from other users (extended facility).

16. After performing Exercise 15, you discover that Tanya (login name `tanya`) has mailed a message to you and four other users. Now, send a reply to Tanya and the other four.

17. Log into a neighboring UNIX system on the `uucp` network called `gemini`.

18. Log into `gemini` and capture your remote session in a file in your working directory called `gemini.session`.

19. Send a message to Ken (login name `ken`) on neighboring UNIX system `minerva`.

20. Print a report called `sales.3Q` on a printer on the `minerva` system.

152

Chapter 7

Formatting Text

What You Will Learn

This chapter introduces text formatting with the *mm* macro package.
The following topics are covered:

- ▶ Formatting tools available in UNIX
- ▶ How to format paragraphs
- ▶ How to format display text
- ▶ How to format lists
- ▶ How to justify text, skip lines, highlight text, and change
  point size

Formatting UNIX Documents

In Chapter 5 you learned how to create documents and enter text
with the vi editor. You use a different program to format text. In
UNIX, as in mainframe operating systems such as VM, editing and
formatting are separate functions.

The Main Formatting Programs

Formatting for UNIX began in the late 1960s with a "runoff" program from the Massachusetts Institute of Technology (MIT) that was called roff. Joseph Ossanna developed an enhanced version of roff that was called the "new runoff" program, or nroff; then he developed a further enhancement for phototypesetters that was called the "typesetter runoff" program, or troff.

The nroff program (pronounced "en-roff") works with line-printers and daisy-wheel printers, which produce typewriter-like characters having a fixed width. Although nroff includes most of the features of troff, it doesn't have to handle changes in point size and proportional spacing.

The troff program (pronounced "tee-roff") works with typesetting equipment and laser printers, which produce characters having variable widths. This program includes every feature of nroff, plus those that produce font changes and proportional spacing.

Both of these programs, like VM's SCRIPT, employ embedded commands, or *requests*, that have short mnemonic names. Most of these requests begin with periods, like WordStar's dot commands, and many require following arguments.

154

The Other Formatting Programs

Both nroff and troff allow you to build *macros* from the basic requests. Using this built-in macro feature, people have developed several *macro packages* derived from nroff and troff. Focusing on the formatting needs of ordinary users, these macro packages are designed to simplify the job of formatting a document. Three of the most prominent macro packages are the following:

ms	The mainstay of UNIX Version 7
me	The macro package of choice for Berkeley versions of UNIX
mm	The program selected for UNIX System V

 A *macro* is a special command that includes other commands.

In addition to macro packages, other programs can also be used for formatting. Preprocessors handle specialized kinds of text for `nroff` and `troff`, including the following:

`tbl`	Formats tables for both programs
`neqn`	Formats mathematical expressions for `nroff`
`eqn`	Formats mathematical expressions for `troff`

Finally, the following two utilities handle miscellaneous tasks related to formatting:

`checkeq`	Checks usage in material to be formatted by `neqn` or `eqn`
`deroff`	Removes formatting requests from a file, including all those for `nroff`, `troff`, `tbl`, `neqn`, and `eqn`

155

The `mm` *Macro Package*

This chapter concentrates on the `mm` macro package. Formatting a document is accomplished in three general steps:

- ▶ Enter the text with an editor such as `vi`
- ▶ Embed the formatting requests
- ▶ Process the formatted document, using a command line such as one of the following:

```
$ mm [option(s)] file(s)
$ nroff -cm [option(s)] file(s)
$ troff -cm [option(s)] file(s)
```

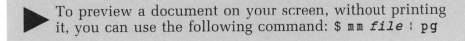

To preview a document on your screen, without printing it, you can use the following command: `$ mm file | pg`

The default printing characteristics for `mm` are as follows:

10 characters per inch (10 cpi, or pica)

6 lines per inch
3/4 inch offset for the left margin
60 characters per line (6 inches)

The following sections describe the individual formatting requests, including those used to take care of paragraphs, display text, lists, highlighting, spacing, and changes in point size. In each example, you will see the formatted document at the left and the printed result at the right.

Formatting Paragraphs

Paragraphs are the basic units in most documents. You have two formatting choices when you use mm, each selected with the .P request. You must precede every paragraph with a separate request. Both types of paragraphs are filled to the current margins.

Forming a Block Paragraph .P 0

To produce a block paragraph, without indentation for the first line, place a .P ▯ (dot P zero) request above the first line.

Original Document	**Printed Result**

```
.P ▯
This is a block paragraph,
with all lines
left-justified. The first
line is unindented.
```

```
This is a block paragraph,
with all lines left-justified.
The first line is unindented.
```

Forming an Indented Paragraph .P 1

To produce an indented paragraph, with the first line indented, place a .P ⅼ (dot P one) request above the first line.

Original Document	Printed Result

`.P 1`
`This is an indented`
`paragraph, which`
`begins with an`
`indented line. The rest`
`of the lines are`
`flush left.`
	`This is an indented`
	`paragraph, which begins with`
	`an indented line. The rest of`
	`the lines are flush left.`

Formatting Display Text

157

You can display text on the printed page by setting it apart with various combinations of spacing, indentation, and centering. With mm, you have four formats to choose from, depending on what you want to display. You can also select between a *static* display and a *floating* display. Both types of display move text to the next page if it doesn't fit on the current page. The difference is that a floating display allows subsequent text to flow ahead of the display into the gap left on the previous page. The basic commands for setting up displays are as follows:

`.DS`	Begin a static display
`.DF`	Begin a floating display
`.DE`	End either type of display

The examples that follow use the `.DS` request. However, you can substitute the `.DF` request on any line in which you see `.DS`.

Forming an Indented Display   *.DS I*

To indent display text five spaces, you can include the I (indent) argument with the `.DS` (or `.DF`) request, as shown below:

Original Document	**Printed Result**
.P ㄥ	
Here is an example of a quotation that is set apart as display text:	Here is an example of a quotation that is set apart as display text:
.DS I	
"I'm mad as hell and I'm not going to take this any more."	"I'm mad as hell and I'm not going to take this any more."
.DE	
.P ㄥ	With these words, Howard Beale concluded his broadcast in "Network."
With these words, Howard Beale concluded his broadcast in "Network."	

158

Forming a Double-Indented Display .DS I F n

If you want the display text indented from both margins, include the I (indent) argument, the F (fill) argument, and a number *n* to indicate how many spaces you want to indent from the right margin. The following example requests an indentation of five spaces from the right margin:

Original Document	**Printed Result**
.P ㄥ	
Here is an example of a quotation that is set apart as display text:	Here is an example of a quotation that is set apart as display text:
.DS I F 5	
"I'm mad as hell and I'm not going to take this any more."	"I'm mad as hell and I'm not going to take this any more."
.DE	
.P ㄥ	With these words, Howard Beale concluded his broadcast in "Network."
With these words, Howard Beale concluded his broadcast in "Network."	

Forming a Centered Display   *.DS C*

For a title or for verses of poetry, you may want to center your display text. Merely include the C (center) argument with your .DS (or .DF) request, as follows:

Original Document	**Printed Result**

```
.P 1
He quoted from the
work named below:
.DS C
"Flying High"
by
Jerry Jett
.DE
.P 1
Then he went on to
discuss the importance
of air safety.
```

```
      He quoted from the work
named below:


            "Flying High"
                 by
            Jerry Jett

      Then he went on to
discuss the importance of air
safety.
```

159

Forming a Blocked Display   *.DS CB*

A variation of the centered display is the blocked display, in which the text is centered with left-justification. For this style, include the CB (center block) argument with your .DS (or .DF) request, as shown in this example:

Original Document	**Printed Result**

```
.P 1
He quoted from "The Fly" by
William Blake:
.DS CB
Am not I
A fly like thee?
Or art not thou
A man like me?
```

```
      He quoted from "The Fly"
by William Blake:

         Am not I
         A fly like thee?
         Or art not thou
         A man like me?
```

```
.DE
.P 1                              Then he went on to quote
Then he went on to quote          from Robert Burns and other
from Robert Burns and             poets.
other poets.
```

Formatting Lists

You can set up a list of items in any of several different styles with `mm`. Each item can begin with a bullet, a hyphen, a letter, a number, or a word. There is a different `mm` request for each type of list; however, you must precede each item with `.LI` (list item) and end every list with the `.LE` (list end) request. The examples that follow illustrate six different types of lists.

160

Forming a Bullet List   *.BL*

To precede each item in your list with a bullet, use the `.BL` (bullet list) request. Under `nroff`, the bullets are simulated (as plus signs); under `troff`, the bullets are real. Here is an example:

Original Document   **Printed Result**

```
.P 1
The steps to produce a              The steps to produce a
formatted document are              formatted document are as
as follows:                         follows:
.BL
.LI                                     + Enter the text with vi
Enter the text with vi
.LI                                     + Enter the formatting
Embed the formatting                      requests
requests
.LI                                     + Process the file with mm
Process the file with mm
.LE
```

Forming a Dash List .DL

To precede each item in your list with a hyphen (not a dash)
rather than a bullet, use the `.DL` (dash list) request, as follows:

Original Document	**Printed Result**

```
.P 1
The steps to produce a
formatted document are
as follows:
.DL
.LI
Enter the text with vi
.LI
Embed the formatting
requests
.LI
Process the file with mm
.LE
```

```
The steps to produce a
formatted document are as
follows:

  - Enter the text with vi

  - Enter the formatting
    request

  - Process the file with mm
```

161

Forming a Mark List .ML

If you want to select a character (or a sequence of characters) to
precede each item, use the `.ML` (mark list) request, with the char-
acter(s) following the request. In the following example, we'll
request an asterisk (∗) in front of each item in the list:

Original Document	**Printed Result**

```
.P 1
The steps to produce a
formatted document are
as follows:
.ML *
.LI
Enter the text with vi
.LI
```

```
The steps to produce a
formatted document are as
follows:

  * Enter the text with vi

  * Enter the formatting requests
```

```
Embed the formatting          * Process the file with mm
requests
.LI
Process the file with mm
.LE
```

Forming a Reference List   .RL

If you want to list references by number (such as a list of sources
for quotations), use the .RL (reference list) request. The results
will be similar to the results in the previous three examples, but
the items will be automatically numbered (within brackets) in
sequence:

162

Original Document	**Printed Result**

```
.P 1
The sources for quotations        The sources for quotations
cited in this book are            cited in this book are as
as follows:                       follows:
.RL
.LI
Arthur, Quinlan P., "New      [1] Arthur, Quinlan P., "New
Ways, New Winds"                  Ways,
.LI                               New Winds"
Betters, Anne G., "Get        [2] Betters, Anne G., "Get
What You Want"                    What You Want"

.LI                           [3] Childress, Layne R.,
Childress, Layne R., "Why         "Why Not Be a Winner?"
Not Be a Winner?"
.LE
```

Forming a Variable-Item List   .VL

If you want to list definitions or explanations with a different term
at the beginning of each item, use the .VL (variable-item list)
request. After the .VL request, you must provide a number that

indicates how many columns you need between the current left margin and the starting column for each definition or explanation. Note that this number must be at least two more than the length of the longest term in the list. (The following example uses 10.)

After each `.LI` request, you have to type the term for that item. This term is what varies from item to item (along with the definition or explanation that follows).

Original Document	**Printed Result**

```
.P 1
The preprocessors for mm,
nroff, and troff are as
follows:
.VL 10
.LI tbl
Formats tables for nroff
and troff
.LI neqn
Formats equations for
nroff
.LI eqn
Formats equations for
troff
.LE
```

```
    The preprocessors for mm,
nroff, and troff are as follows:

tbl    Formats tables for
       nroff and troff

neqn   Formats equations for
       nroff

eqn    Formats equations for
       troff
```

163

Forming an Auto-Number List   *.AL*

In its simplest form, an *auto-number* list is similar to a reference list. Each item is numbered sequentially, beginning at 1. However, the `.AL` (auto-number list) request has additional options and is much more versatile. Following is an example of a simple `.AL` request without options:

Original Document	**Printed Result**

```
.P 1
The sources for quotations
cited in this book are
as follows:
```

```
    The sources for quotations
cited in this book are as
follows:
```

```
.AL
.LI                              1.  Arthur, Quinlan P., "New
Arthur, Quinlan P., "New             Ways, New Winds"
Ways, New Winds"
.LI                              2.  Betters, Anne G., "Get
Betters, Anne G., "Get               What You Want"
What You Want"
.LI                              3.  Childress, Layne R.,
Childress, Layne R., "Why            "Why Not Be a Winner?"
Not Be a Winner?"
.LE
```

In the preceding example, the results are similar to the results for `.VL`. However, you can also request Roman numerals or letters rather than Arabic numbers. Merely type one of the following options after the `.AL` request to select the appropriate numbering scheme:

A   Uppercase LETTERS
a   Lowercase letters
I   Uppercase Roman NUMERALS
i   Lowercase Roman numerals

The following example selects uppercase letters:

<table>
<tr><th>Original Document</th><th>Printed Result</th></tr>
</table>

```
.P 1
The main topics to be                The main topics to be
addressed tonight are                addressed tonight are as
as follows:                          follows:
.AL A
.LI                              A.  Making new contacts
Making new contacts
.LI                              B.  Cultivating new ideas
Cultivating new ideas
.LI                              C.  Signing contracts
Signing contracts
.LE
```

By nesting `.AL` requests, you can construct an outline. Just use `I` for the first `.AL` request, `A` for the second, `1` for the third, and so on. The numbering for a given level remains in effect until the `.LE` request that ends the list. Here is an example of an outline:

Original Document	**Printed Result**

```
.AL I     [Start of Roman list]
.LI
Setup
.AL A     [Start of "ABC" list]
.LI
Introduce Dorothy
.LI
Introduce the others:
.AL 1     [Start of "123" list]
.LI
Aunt and uncle
.LI
Farm hands
.LI
Mean neighbor
.LI
County fair charlatan
.LE       [End of "123" list]
.LI
Describe Dorothy's desire
to get away
.LI
Cyclone sequence ends Act I
.LE       [End of "ABC" list]
.LI
Chase: the quest for
the wizard
...
.LI
Payoff: the return home

...
.LE       [End of Roman list]
```

```
  I. Setup

     A.  Introduce Dorothy

     B.  Introduce the
         others:

         1.  Aunt and
             uncle

         2.  Farm hands

         3.  Mean
             neighbor

         4.  County fair
             charlatan

     C.  Describe Dorothy's
         desire to get away

     D.  Cyclone sequence
         ends Act I

 II.  Chase: the quest for the
      wizard

      ...

III.  Payoff: the return home

      ...
```

165

Other Formatting Features

This section discusses the `mm` requests for justifying text, skipping lines, highlighting text, and changing the point size of characters.

Justifying Text   *.SA*

By default, `mm` causes text to be printed flush left, but not flush right. To produce justification along the right margin, use the `.SA 1` request. To turn off justification and return to the default, use the `.SA 0` request. The following example uses both requests:

166

Original Document	**Printed Result**

```
.SA 1
.P 1
This paragraph will be
printed flush left and
flush right. Each line
will be adjusted as
required.
.SA 0
.P 1
This paragraph will be
printed flush left and
ragged right. Lines
will be filled but not
justified.
```

```
    This  paragraph  will   be
printed  flush  left  and flush
right.  Each   line   will   be
adjusted as required.


    This paragraph will be
printed flush left and ragged
right. Lines will be filled but
not justified.
```

Skipping Lines   *.SP n*

You can create blank space on a page by leaving a specified number of blank lines between segments of text. Use the `.SP` request, followed by a number, as shown in the following example. In this example, we'll leave three blank lines.

Original Document	Printed Result

```
.P 1
This paragraph will be
printed in its expected
location on the page.
.SP 3
.P 1
This paragraph will be
printed three lines
lower than the
previous paragraph.
```

```
     This paragraph will be
printed in its expected
location on the page.



     This paragraph will be
printed three lines lower than
the previous paragraph.
```

Highlighting Text

167

To allow you to highlight words in a paragraph, `mm` provides one request for italic text (`.I`), one for bold (`.B`), and one for returning to unhighlighted, or roman, text (`.R`). (Under `nroff`, italic means underscoring; under `troff`, italic means true italic.)

For more than one word, enclose the target text between a pair of requests, using three separate lines. The first line contains the highlighting request (`.I` or `.B`), the middle line contains the text to be highlighted, and the third line contains `.R` and nothing else. For a single word, you can issue the request on a single line. During printing, `mm` will restore the paragraph, which appears to be broken up by this procedure.

The following example illustrates each of the possibilities mentioned:

Original Document	Printed Result

```
.P 1
When you want a word to be
.I underlined
, merely use the .I request.
To underline
.I
several words
.R
, use .I and .R together.
```

```
     When you want a word to
be underlined, merely use the
.I request. To underline
several words, use .I and .R
together.

     When you want a word in
bold, just use the .B
```

```
.P 1
When you want a word in          request. To make several
.B bold                          words bold, use .B and .R
, just use the .B request.       together
To make
.B
several words
.R
bold, use .B and .R together.
```

Changing Point Size   *.S p v*

When you are formatting mm requests with troff, you can change
the size of the characters being printed and the amount of spacing
between lines of text. The .S request can be used to change one of
these measurements, or both at the same time. Let's begin with a
description of point size and vertical spacing.

The size of a printed character is measured in *points* (1/72s of
an inch). Actually the size is for a set of characters and is defined
as the distance from the bottom of a lowercase "p" to the top of
any uppercase letter. For reference, 9 points equal an eighth of an
inch, 12 points equal a sixth of an inch, 18 points equal a quarter
of an inch, and so on.

Vertical spacing is the distance, also measured in points, from
the bottom of one line to the bottom of the next line. In most
books, vertical spacing is about 20% greater than point size. The
difference, in points, between the vertical spacing and the point
size is known as the *leading* (pronounced to rhyme with
"heading").

For troff, the default is 10-point text and 12-point vertical
spacing (2-point leading). The .S request can be used with either
one argument or two arguments: point size and vertical spacing.
You can enter a pair of numbers to express absolute sizes in
points, you can enter numbers to express relative sizes, or you can
enter a single letter from the following list:

C   Current settings

D   Default settings

P   Previous settings (equivalent to no argument at all)

In the following example, the size is increased for a title, decreased once for a byline, and then restored to the default sizes for the main body of text:

Original Document	**Printed Result**

```
.SP 3
.DS C
.S 14 18
The Big Thrill
.S -2 -4
By Henry Harker
.DE
.S D
.P 0
It wasn't a dark and stormy
night. It wasn't even night.
It was what you might call a
bright and sunny day. In fact,
that's just what it was.
```

```
The Big Thrill

By Henry Harker

It wasn't a dark and stormy
night. It wasn't even night.
It was what you might call a
bright and sunny day. In fact,
that's just what it was.
```

169

Here is a detailed look at the seven mm requests used in the previous example:

`.SP 3`	Leave three blank lines
`.DS C`	Start a centered display
`.S 14 18`	Change the point size to 14 and the vertical spacing to 18
`.S -2 -4`	Reduce the point size by 2 points and the vertical spacing by 4 (equivalent to .S 12 14)
`.DS E`	End the centered display
`.S D`	Restore the default settings for point size and vertical spacing (equivalent to .S 10 12)
`.P 0`	Begin a block paragraph

What You've Learned

This chapter showed you how to format text with the `mm` macro package. First, you learned the names of the programs that handle formatting in UNIX: `nroff`, `troff`, `tbl`, `neqn`, `eqn`, `checkeq`, and `deroff`. Then, you learned the steps required to produce formatted pages of text: enter the text, embed the formatting requests, and process the file with one of the formatters.

The `mm` macro package lets you form either blocked paragraphs (`.P 0`) or paragraphs with indented first lines (`.P 1`). You can use either a static display (`.DS`) or a floating display (`.DF`) to set up one of four formats for displays: indented, double-indented, centered, or blocked.

You can set up any one of six different types of lists: bullet (`.BL`), dash (`.DL`), mark (`.ML`), reference (`.RL`), variable-item (`.VL`), or auto-numbered (`.AL`). You can also either justify text (`.SA 1`) or unjustify it (`.SA 0`); skip *n* lines (`.SP n`); make text italic (`.I`), bold (`.B`), or roman (`.R`); or change point size and line spacing (`.S p v`).

170

Chapter 7 Quiz

Match the name of the program listed on the left with the description of its function on the right:

1. `deroff`	A. Format text for a printer with characters having a fixed width
2. `checkeq`	B. Format text for a printer with characters having variable widths
3. `troff`	C. Process tables
4. `eqn`	D. Process equations for the `nroff` formatter
5. `neqn`	E. Process equations for the `troff` formatter
6. `nroff`	F. Check requests used in equations and mathematical expressions
7. `tbl`	G. Remove formatting requests from a file

Match the name of each `mm` request listed on the left with the description of its function on the right:

8. `.DE`		A.	Form a block paragraph
9. `.RL`		B.	Form a paragraph with an indented first line
10. `.P 0`		C.	Begin a static display
11. `.SA 0`		D.	Begin a floating display
12. `.DL`		E.	End a text display
13. `.S`		F.	Begin an indented static display
14. `.EL`		G.	Begin a centered floating display
15. `.B`		H.	Begin a blocked floating display
16. `.P 1`		I.	Begin a bullet list
17. `.R`		J.	Begin a dash list
18. `.SP` n		K.	Begin a mark list
19. `.DS`		L.	Begin a reference list
20. `.AL`		M.	Begin a variable-item list
21. `.I`		N.	Begin an auto-number list
22. `.DF`		O.	Begin an individual item in a list
23. `.ML`		P.	End a list
24. `.DS I`		Q.	Begin italic (or underscored) text
25. `.SA 1`		R.	Begin bold text
26. `.LI`		S.	End bold or italic text
27. `.VL`		T.	Turn on justification
28. `.DF CB`		U.	Turn off justification
29. `.BL`		V.	Skip n lines
30. `.DF C`		W.	Change the point size and vertical spacing

171

In the blank spaces provided after the numbers on the left, fill in the `mm` formatting requests needed to produce the printed output shown on the right:

Original Document	Printed Result
31.	Sales 1991
32.	
Sales 1991	Mr. Downs was introduced to the sales staff on Friday morning. During his talk, he stressed the following points:
33.	
34.	
35.	
Mr. Downs was introduced to the sales staff on Friday morning. During his talk, he stressed the following points:	
36.	+ Finding prospects
37.	
Finding prospects	+ Reaching prospects
38.	
Reaching prospects	+ Closing prospects
39.	
Closing prospects	He stressed the value of new referrals over and over. At one point he was quoted as saying,
40.	
41.	
He stressed the value of new referrals over and over. At one point he was quoted as saying,	
42.	"Get those referrals, no matter what you have to do. **Get those referrals!**"
"Get those referrals, no matter what you have to do.	
43.	
Get those referrals	
44.	
!"	The following Monday, sales wer up *27%*. Mr. Downs was highly pleased, and informed the staff that he would give another talk the following Friday.
45.	
46.	
The following Monday, sales were up	
47. 27%	
. Mr. Downs was highly pleased, and informed the staff that he would give another talk the following Friday.	

172

System Administration

What You Will Learn

This chapter explains the basic operations needed for administering a UNIX system, including:

- ▶ What a system administrator does
- ▶ Setting up new user accounts
- ▶ Finding out who is logged in
- ▶ Backing up files
- ▶ Setting up terminals
- ▶ Running processes automatically
- ▶ Using numeric permissions
- ▶ Shutting the system down

The System Administrator

If you have been using DOS for any length of time, you probably know that you must perform certain "housekeeping" tasks in order to use your system effectively. You have to format disks, make backup copies of files, prune directories from time to time, and maintain the integrity of files.

With UNIX, your administrative tasks are quite a bit more complex. You have user accounts to administer; you have terminals, printers, and disk and tape drives to set up; you have file systems to maintain; and you have permissions to grant or revoke. We won't be able to cover all these tasks in this chapter, but we will take a look at the most common and least technical of these. Let's begin with a quick look at the responsibilities of a system administrator.

What a System Administrator Does

174

When you work with DOS, you are both the user and the system administrator. You run your programs and back up your own disk files. In a UNIX system with many users, someone is usually assigned the task of supporting these users in their day-to-day work by handling the administrative tasks for everyone. This system administrator is responsible for the following:

Opening and closing user accounts on the system

Installing, mounting, and troubleshooting terminals, printers, plotters, disk drives, and tape drives

Providing sufficient disk space and keeping file systems free of errors

Formatting disks, starting the system, and shutting it down

Protecting the system from unauthorized entry and destructive actions

Monitoring system usage to guard against attacks, to optimize the performance of the system, and to handle billing

Setting up connections to other UNIX systems

Now, let's examine the tools available to the system administrator for carrying out these responsibilities.

Logging In as System Administrator

If you are currently logged into your system as an ordinary user, then you can switch to system administrator by logging in again with the su (substitute user) command, as follows:

```
$ su
Password:
# _
```

If you are not currently logged in, you can log into the root account, which is reserved for the system administrator:

```
login: root
Password:
# _
```

175

In either case, the shell displays a special prompt (#) to remind you that you are no longer logged in as an ordinary user. You are now logged in as the system's *super user*. (That's much like the transformation that takes place when Clark Kent emerges from a telephone booth as Superman.)

The super user has complete access to every directory, every subdirectory, and every file in the system, without having to worry about permissions. There is nothing to stop you from entering any directory and creating or deleting any file. If you make a mistake, you can damage a system beyond repair. Therefore, only one person should be allowed to log in as super user—and only when required to perform system maintenance.

In no instance should super user status be given to someone who is likely to misuse the privilege. Select a super user who is diligent and knowledgeable, and who maintains the highest standards of professional ethics.

The System Administrator's Directory /etc

Most administrative files and commands are stored in a separate directory called /etc. Separating administrative commands from the ordinary commands in /bin and /usr/bin keeps these special commands out of the hands of other users. You can always type the full pathname of any command; however, if you want to be able to use only the command name, place one of the following in your start-up file .profile (Bourne shell) or .login (C shell):

Bourne shell
```
PATH=/etc:/bin:/usr/bin:$HOME/bin:
export PATH
```

C shell
```
set path = (/etc /bin /usr/bin $HOME/bin .)
```

With one of these lines in your start-up file, you will be free to enter commands by their basenames, without having to type full pathnames.

176

Working with Users

One of the important jobs of a system administrator is to interact with system users. In this section, you will learn how to communicate with users, how to set up new user accounts, and how to determine who is logged in at any given moment.

Reaching Users

Because the users on your UNIX system may not be in the same room, or even in the same building, you need an efficient way to get information to them at various times. The mail command may be a little too slow, so UNIX offers three other possibilities: the wall (write-all) command, the news command, and the /etc/motd (message of the day) file.

The wall (write-all) command is similar to the write command, in that it immediately sends a message to each terminal. Although this is the fastest way to reach users, your message will be seen only by users who are currently logged in. So, another possibility is to use the news command, which displays the contents of files stored in /usr/news.

Another option is the /etc/motd (message of the day) file. Any announcement placed in this file will be displayed each time a user logs in. Here is an example of a typical message of the day:

```
The system will be shut down
Friday night at 10:00 pm.
```

To display this message, merely change to the directory /etc, use vi to begin an editing session with the file motd, replace the current message of the day with the new message, and save the text.

Users can reply to messages from the system administrator or send their own messages to the system administrator by mailing them to root, as shown in the following example:

```
$ mail root < lost.files
$ _
```

177

Setting Up New User Accounts

Information about each user authorized to log into a UNIX system is summarized as a one-line entry in a file called /etc/passwd. Each entry contains seven fields, separated from each other by colons (:):

Login name

Password (encrypted)

User identifier

Group identifier (optional)

Comments, such as full name (optional)

Home directory

Login program (usually a shell)

The system will associate the user identifier and the group identifier (if any) with each file that the user creates. A typical /etc/passwd file looks something like this:

```
root:uR@pwCyI5z:0:1:super user:/:
daemon:x:1:1::/:
cron:x:1:3::/:
sys:nQ3vB*eJ4:2:2:/sys:
bin:k8S(oL7gYb:3:2::/bin:
paul:Z.u3)qKf9:15:62:Paul Stafford:/usr/paul:/bin/sh
...
```

The sixth entry can be broken down as follows:

Field	Entry	Description
1	paul	Login name
2	Z.u3)qKf9	Password (encrypted)
3	15	User identifier
4	62	Group identifier
5	Paul Stafford	Comment (full name)
6	/usr/paul	Home directory
7	/bin/sh	Login program (Bourne shell)

Each working group on the system is described as a one-line entry in a file called /etc/group. With only four fields, this file is a little simpler than /etc/passwd:

Group name

Password (encrypted)

Group identifier

List of members

A typical /etc/group file looks something like this:

```
root:uR@pwCyI5z:1:root,deamon
sys:nQ3vB*eJ4:2:sys,bin
family:jYp4+sK&m:61:archie,edith,gloria,mike
...
```

The third line can be broken down as follows:

Field	Entry	Description
1	family	Group name
2	jYp4+sK&m	Password (encrypted)
3	61	Group identifier
4	archie,edith,gloria,mike	List of members

To add a new user account to the system, you must perform the following operations as super user:

- ▶ Add a line to /etc/passwd
- ▶ Add a line to /etc/group (if necessary)
- ▶ Provide the user with a home directory
- ▶ Construct a start-up file

179

Here are the steps in detail:

1. Add a line to the system password file:
   ▶ Begin editing at the end of /etc/passwd:

   `# vi + /etc/passwd`

    Use a plus sign between a `vi` command and a file-name to begin a session at the end of the file.

   ▶ Append a line for the new user:

   ```
   a
   paul:[password]:15:62:Paul Stafford:/usr/paul:/bin/sh
   Esc
   ```

   For the C shell, make the last field /bin/csh instead of /bin/sh.

▶ End this editing session and return to the shell:

```
:wq
# _
```

2. Provide the user with a home directory:

▶ Create the home directory in /usr:

```
# cd /usr
# mkdir paul
# _
```

▶ Change the name of the directory's owner from root to paul:

```
# chown paul paul
# _
```

▶ Assuming the user belongs to group 62, change the owner's group identifier to 62:

```
# chgrp 62 /usr/paul
# _
```

3. Create a start-up file in the new directory:

▶ Log into the new directory:

```
# login paul
Password:
# _
```

▶ Begin an editing session with vi and the start-up file:

```
$ vi + .profile      [Bourne shell]
```

For the C shell, use .login instead of .profile, and use the appropriate corresponding lines.

▶ Specify pathnames for commands and mail:

```
a
PATH=:/lbin:/usr/bin:/usr/paul/bin:
MAIL=/usr/mail/paul
```

▶ Identify and set the user's terminal:

```
TERM=tv950
stty erase '^h' kill '^u'
```

▶ Export the variables (Bourne shell only):

```
export PATH, MAIL, TERM
Esc
```

▶ End this editing session and return to the shell prompt:

```
:wq
# _
```

180

Finding Out Who Is Logged In   *who*

One of the simplest security measures you can perform is to check
periodically to find out which users are currently logged in. To do
so, use the who command, as illustrated here:

```
$ who
root           tty00          May  2 08:59
alexis         tty05          May  2 09:23
ted            tty21          May  2 11:15
bill           tty02          Apr 29 04:26
paul           tty20          May  2 10:21
nancy          tty03          Apr 30 10:37
toad           tty26          May  2 11:42
$ _
```

181

The who command reads login information from a file called
/etc/utmp and displays it as shown above. Each line of the who
display specifies the login name of a user, the name of the terminal, and the date and time when the user logged in.

If you would like more information, you can use the –u argument to obtain a long listing:

```
$ who -u
root           tty00          May  2 08:59    .     19457
alexis         tty05          May  2 09:23  2:09    22344
ted            ttym1          May  2 11:15    .     26510
bill           tty02          Apr 29 04:26  1:22       44
paul           ttym0          May  2 10:21  2:01    26322
nancy          tty03          Apr 30 10:37  1:48     1155
toad           ttym6          May  2 11:42    .     26755
$ _
```

This long listing includes two additional columns at the right:
the amount of time since the user's last activity and the process
identifier (PID) of the user's shell. In the time column, each value
is given in hours and minutes; two other notations include a dot
(.), indicating activity within the last minute, and old, meaning
no activity in the past 24 hours.

If you would like a complete listing of lines currently available on your system (not currently in use), you can include the –l
argument, as follows:

```
$ who -l
LOGIN       tty01           May  2 22:21  1:22  26362
LOGIN       tty07           Apr 29 16:25  old      49
LOGIN       tty08           Apr 29 16:25  old      50
LOGIN       tty09           May  2 10:13 13:29  22338
LOGIN       tty10           Apr 29 20:16  old     913
LOGIN       tty06           Apr 29 16:25  old      48
LOGIN       tty11           Apr 29 20:16  old     912
LOGIN       tty12           Apr 30 21:30  old    6438
LOGIN       tty24           May  2 23:38  5:23  26746
LOGIN       tty27           May  2 23:39 15:12  26756
LOGIN       tty25           May  2 23:40  0:03  26764
LOGIN       tty04           Apr 30 21:31  old    8428
LOGIN       tty16           May  2 20:01  3:42  25722
$ _
```

182

Backing Up Files

One task that you have to perform whether you are using DOS or UNIX is file backup. UNIX provides several commands for backing up files, but we'll focus on only one of them, the cpio (copy input/output) command.

The Copy I/O Program   *cpio*

You can use the cpio command to perform three basic functions:

Copy files (out) to a disk or tape drive

Copy files (in) from a disk or tape drive

Copy files from one directory to another

You use the first function to back up your files; you use the second to recover files from backup; and you use the third to copy files to a different directory. You select these three functions of cpio by including one of the three *keys* in Table 8-1 as an argument to the cpio command.

Table 8-1. `cpio` *Keys*

Key	Function
-o	Output: Copy files from a directory to a backup device
-i	Input: Copy files from a backup device to a directory
-p	Pass: Copy files from a source directory to a target directory

Options *for the* `cpio` *Command*

You can specify several options for `cpio`. Merely bundle the option with the key. Table 8-2 lists the most common options:

Table 8-2. `cpio` *Options*

183

Option	Function
t	Table of contents: Don't copy any files; merely display filenames.
v	Verbose: Display the name of each file as it is being copied.
B	Block: Write to tape in blocks of 5,120 bytes (output and input only).
d	Directory: Create any directories required (input and pass only).
l	Link: Link rather than copy (pass only).

Copying Files Out   *cpio -o*

Part of Paul's home directory is shown in Figure 8-1. For the sake of simplicity, let's assume that the subdirectory called `active` contains two ordinary files and two subdirectories, and that each subdirectory in turn contains three more files.

Suppose you want to back up these files on a tape drive that is identified by the filename `/dev/rmt/2`. Because you are copying from the file system out to a device, you must use the -o (output) key. Because you are copying to tape, you should use blocks, which require the B (blocks) option.

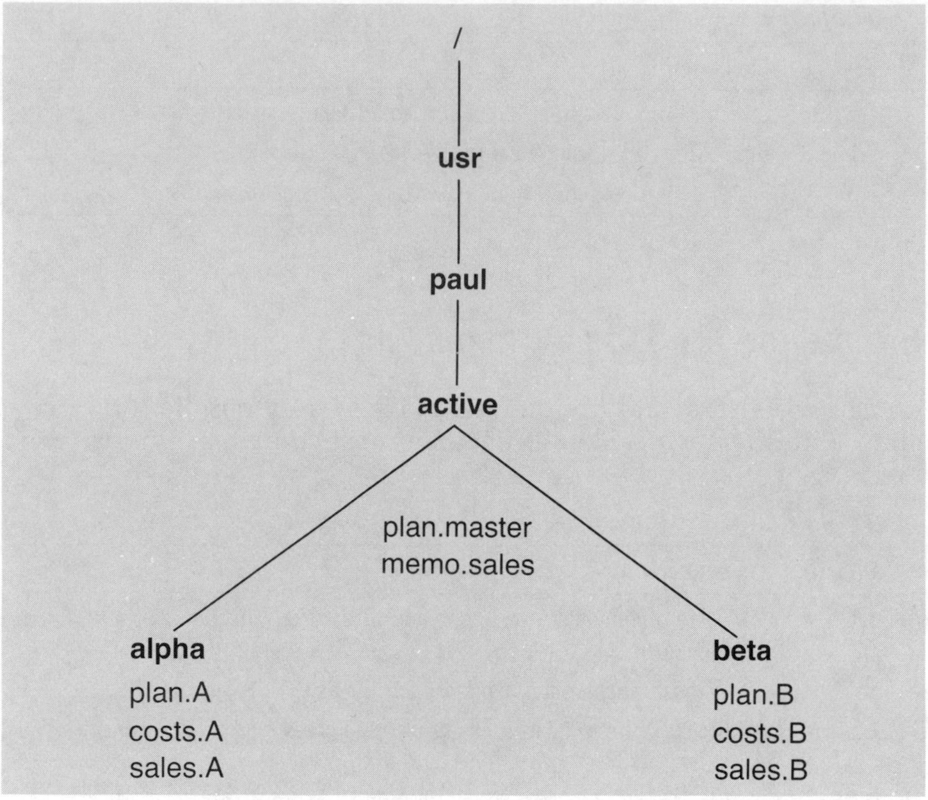

Figure 8-1. A Directory to Be Backed Up

184

To copy only the files in one directory, you can pipe the file-names to the cpio command with the ls command. In the following example, you will copy the two ordinary files in /usr/paul/active (plan.master and memo.sales) to tape:

```
$ pwd
/usr/paul/active
$ ls : cpio -oB > /dev/mt/2
6 blocks
$ _
```

In the preceding example, the ls command provides the names of the files in the directory. The cpio command receives the names through a pipe (:); it then sends the contents out in blocks (-oB), with the output redirected to the desired tape drive

(> /dev/rmt/2). On the following line, the message tells you that six blocks were written.

The previous command copies ordinary files, but it excludes subdirectories. If you want to copy files, subdirectories, and the files within those subdirectories, use find rather than ls, as shown in the following example:

```
$ pwd
/usr/paul
$ find /usr/paul/active -print ¦
cpio - oB > /dev/rmt/2
25 blocks
$ _
```

> In Unix, "print" means "display" or "list." In the find command, -print means the same thing.

In this example, the find command provides the names of all files in the directory /usr/paul/active as input for the cpio command (-print). The rest of the command is the same as in the previous example, except that 25 blocks are written this time. The following example includes the v (verbose) option to list the files being copied:

```
$ pwd
/usr/paul
$ find /usr/paul/active -print ¦
cpio - ovB > /dev/mt/2
/usr/paul/active/alpha/plan.A
/usr/paul/active/alpha/costs.A
/usr/paul/active/alpha/sales.A
/usr/paul/active/alpha
/usr/paul/active/alpha/plan.B
/usr/paul/active/alpha/costs.B
/usr/paul/active/alpha/sales.B
/usr/paul/active/beta
/usr/paul/active/plan.master
/usr/paul/active/memo.sales
25 blocks
$ _
```

A thorough backup, like the preceding one, includes the entire contents of the directory. If you should have to recover from errors, you can restore directory /usr/paul/active exactly as it was.

Copying Files In   *cpio -i*

The input key (-i) is used to recover files that have been previously backed up using the output key (-o), which is described in the preceding subsection. Suppose an error has occurred in the file system and you must recover the files that you backed up on tape in the previous example. You can use the following command line to copy the files back into /usr/paul/active:

```
$ pwd
/usr/paul/active
$ cpio -iB < /dev/rmt/2
$ _
```

In this example, the cpio command takes its input from the tape drive (< /dev/rmt/2) and copies it into the current directory with blocking retained (-iB).

If your original backup was to a disk drive, you would not have used blocks. Therefore, when you restore the files, you can omit the B option. Here is an example of restoring files from a disk drive:

```
$ pwd
/usr/paul/active
$ cpio -i < /dev/rdsk/c0d2s1
$ _
```

This example is nearly the same as the previous example. The only two differences are the absence of the block option (B) and the name of the disk device (/dev/rdsk/c0d2s1). The name of the special file that represents the disk device incorporates the identifiers for the disk controller (c0), the disk (d2), and the *slice* (s1). Together, they form the name (c0d2s1). (Note that "slice" is another name for "partition.")

Passing Files   *cpio -p*

You can use the –p (pass) key to copy files from one directory to
another. You probably wouldn't use this third function of cpio for
a backup, but it does give you an additional choice. Passing files
is similar to copying files out, except that the target is a directory
in the file system instead of a device.

Suppose you want to copy files from /usr/paul/active to
/usr/paul/archive. If you want to copy only ordinary files, not
subdirectories or the contents of subdirectories, you can use a
command like this:

```
$ pwd
/usr/paul/active
$ ls ¦ cpio -pv ../archive
/usr/paul/active/plan.master
/usr/paul/active/memo.sales
6 blocks
$ _
```

In the preceding example, cpio receives its input
from ls through a pipe and passes it to the directory
/usr/paul/archive. The v (verbose) option causes the
names of the files to be displayed.

If you want to include all files in the current directory and all
its subdirectories, you can use something like the following:

```
$ pwd
/usr/paul/active
$ find . -print ¦ cpio -pv ../archive
/usr/paul/active/alpha/plan.A
/usr/paul/active/alpha/costs.A
/usr/paul/active/alpha/sales.A
/usr/paul/active/alpha
/usr/paul/active/alpha/plan.B
/usr/paul/active/alpha/costs.B
/usr/paul/active/alpha/sales.B
/usr/paul/active/beta
/usr/paul/active/plan.master
/usr/paul/active/memo.sales
25 blocks
$ _
```

In the preceding example, the `find` command provides a list of names in the current directory (.) and pipes the list to `cpio`. This time, all files in the directory and its subdirectories are copied to `/usr/paul/archive`.

Other Backup Programs

In this section, we've restricted our discussion of backup and recovery to `cpio`. However, there are also several other programs that you can use. Table 8-3 offers a brief summary of these other programs.

Table 8-3. Backup and Recovery Programs

Program	Comments
dd	A copy program that allows you to convert files from one format or standard to another.
tar	Tape archive: the predecessor of `cpio`, which is a little easier to use, but less versatile.
dump	A backup program that allows nine dump levels from 0 (entire system) to 9 (most recently changed files). Caution: `dump` is incapable of detecting end of tape.
restor	Counterpart of `dump`, used to restore from backup. Caution: it is difficult to select individual files with `restor`.
volcopy	Volume copy: copies an entire file system, but not individual files, to disk or tape.

The `cpio` command is probably your best choice for backup and recovery because of its flexibility and versatility. When you use `find` to filter filenames for it, `cpio` can pinpoint the files to be copied with great precision.

Setting Up Terminals

In this section, we'll take a look at the methods for describing the behavior and functions of a terminal to UNIX. UNIX must have a description of each terminal that is connected to the system.

Basic Terminal Settings   *stty*

Intercommunication between a terminal and a computer depends on agreement between the two on several communication traits: transmission speed, parity, word length, and so on. Default settings for these traits are stored for each terminal in a file called /etc/gettydefs. You can display the settings for your terminal by using the stty (set terminal) command. Much of what you will see displayed is beyond the scope of this book, so we'll confine our discussion to a few important items. If you use the stty command without any arguments, you will see something like this:

```
$ stty
speed 1200 baud; -parity
erase = ^h; kill = ^u;
...
$ _
```

Here is a summary of the four items displayed above:

speed 1200 baud	The terminal transmits and receives at 1200 bits per second.
-parity	Turn off parity detection, or error-checking, and set character size to 8 bits.
erase = ^h	The key combination for erasing the character behind the cursor is Ctrl-H (abbreviated as ^h).
kill = ^u	The key combination for erasing a command line is Ctrl-U (abbreviated as ^u).

By executing stty with arguments, you can change any of the settings for your terminal. For example, to change the speed, or transmission rate, to 2400 bits per second, use the following command:

```
$ stty 2400
$ _
```

The valid rates for this command are 50, 75, 110, 134, 150, 200, 300, 600, 1200, 1800, 2400, 4800, 9600, and 19200. The rate for your terminal must always match the rate for the host computer or modem.

If you want to enable parity detection for your terminal, you can use the following:

```
$ stty parity
$ _
```

If necessary, you can change more than one setting on a single command line, as illustrated in the next example:

```
$ stty 2400 parity
$ _
```

Keep in mind that stty does not change the settings of your terminal; it merely informs UNIX of these settings. On older terminals, you change actual terminal settings by flipping DIP switches. On newer terminals, you make actual changes by selecting items from a screen menu. In any event, the host computer settings remain constant. You must change the settings on your terminal to match those of the computer.

As illustrated in the previous examples, certain settings can be turned on (parity) or turned off (-parity) with a pair of similar arguments. The hyphen, or minus sign, indicates that the feature is off. Here's one more example:

raw	Allow "raw" input
-raw	Allow "cooked" input

These options affect the way the system accepts information that you enter from your keyboard (the input device for your terminal). Raw means the system accepts exactly what you type, corrections and all; cooked means that the corrections are incorporated before the system sees them. For example, suppose you begin a command line by typing sotr, back up and erase tr, and then correct the name by typing rt. Now you see sort on the command line, but what does the system see? Here is the answer:

sotr^h^hrt	If you have selected raw input, the system sees this.
sort	If you have selected cooked input, the system see this (the default).

Most users need the cooked, or −raw, option. However, the raw option is also available for system programmers and troubleshooters.

Describing Full-Screen Features

Any time you use a program like vi, which requires a full-screen display, the system must have a description of your terminal in another file. Until a few years ago, that file was called /etc/termcap. However, AT&T introduced a replacement for /etc/termcap when it released System V—a directory called /usr/lib/terminfo. The description of your terminal must be in one of these two places.

In the termcap (terminal capability) file, all terminal descriptions are in a single large file. However, terminfo (terminal information) is a directory, which contains subdirectories named after letters of the alphabet. A subdirectory named a contains all the descriptions for terminals with names that begin with the letter "a"; b contains the entries for terminals whose names start with the letter "b"; and so on.

Let's examine a sample entry for termcap; then, let's look at the corresponding entry for terminfo. One of the simplest terminals to describe is the Lear Siegler ADM-3. This is what the description of the ADM-3 looks like in termcap:

191

```
l3|adm3|3|lsi adm3:bs:am:li#24:co#80:cl=^Z
```

The first four items, which are separated from each other by vertical bars (¦), are the four names that you can use to identify this terminal:

```
l3 (el three, not thirteen)
adm3
3
lsi adm3
```

The remaining five items, which are separated by colons (:), are the codes that are used to identify the terminal's capabilities:

bs	Backspace: it can move the cursor back and erase the previous character.
am	Automargins: when the cursor reaches the right side of the screen, the terminal can wrap it to the next line.
li#24	Number of lines: 24
co#80	Number of columns: 80
cl=∧Z	Clear the screen: you can clear the screen by pressing Ctrl-Z (∧Z).

Next, let's look at the entry for the same terminal (the ADM-3) in /usr/lib/terminfo/a/adm3. (Your system will have one of these entries, but not both.) Note that you won't actually be able to display the terminfo entry, because it has been compiled from an original entry that looks like this:

192

```
13¦adm3¦3¦lsi adm3, cub1=∧H,
am, lines#24, cols#80, clear=∧Z,
cud1=∧J, ind=∧J, cr=∧M, bel=∧G
```

The first four items, mnemonic names for the terminal, are exactly the same as the first four items in the termcap entry. The next five, which are separated from each other by commas, are similar to the corresponding entries in termcap, but not identical. Here is a closer look at them:

cub1=∧H	Backspace: you can move the cursor back and erase the previous character by pressing Ctrl-H (∧H).
am	Automargins: when the cursor reaches the right side of the screen, the terminal can wrap it to the next line.
lines#24	Number of lines: 24
cols#80	Number of columns: 80
clear=∧Z	Clear the screen: you can clear the screen by pressing Ctrl-Z (∧Z).

On the second line, the terminfo entry contains four additional items not found in the termcap entry:

cud1=^J	Cursor down: press Ctrl-J to move the cursor down
ind=^J	Index: equivalent to the previous item
cr=^M	Carriage return: Press Ctrl-M to perform a carriage return
bel=^G	Bell (beep): Press Ctrl-G to sound the beeper

Now, let's compare the two entries side by side:

termcap	terminfo	Description
l3	l3	First name
adm3	adm3	Second name
3	3	Third name
lsi adm3	lsi adm3	Fourth name
bs	cub1=^H	Backspacing
am	am	Automargins
li#24	lines#24	Lines: 24
co#80	cols#80	Columns: 80
cl=^Z	clear=^Z	Clear the screen: Ctrl-Z
	cud1=^J	Cursor down: Ctrl-J
	ind=^J	Index: Ctrl-J
	cr=^M	Carriage return: Ctrl-M
	bel=^G	Bell (beeper): Ctrl-G

193

If you are using an ADM-3 terminal, and you are planning to use vi, then you must first execute one of the following command lines:

Bourne shell	**C shell**
$ TERM=adm3; export TERM	% setenv TERM adm3
$ _	% _

Of course, you can also use any of the other three names for the terminal in place of adm3 (l3, 3, or lsi adm3). Better yet, you can place one of these command lines in your start-up file. Then it will be executed automatically every time you log in. Here is the procedure:

Bourne shell	C shell
`$ cd`	`% cd`
`$ vi + .profile`	`% vi + .login`
`a`	`a`
`TERM=adm3; export TERM`	`setenv TERM adm3`
`Esc`	`Esc`
`:wq`	`:wq`
`$ _`	`% _`

194

The terminal used in the previous examples, the ADM-3, is one of the simplest terminals you can find. Some entries in `termcap` or `terminfo` can go on for thirty or forty lines for powerful, intelligent terminals. A sophisticated terminal such as the DEC VT320 has extensive capabilities for handling text-editing, graphics, and international character sets.

Remember, you can't use `vi` on your terminal until you've done the following:

▶ You have located an entry for your terminal in `termcap` (or `terminfo`).

▶ You have identified your terminal to the system by assigning its name to the shell variable `TERM`.

On many UNIX systems, the system administrator handles these details for each user. However, on a system that has no system administrator, you may have to carry out these steps yourself.

Self-Running Processes

The next two sections discuss self-running processes that run on their own schedules and those processes that you can set on the UNIX system timer.

Daemon Processes

Many of the functions of a UNIX system are carried out by processes that start themselves in the background according to a fixed schedule. These processes, known as *daemons*, are responsible for sending print requests in the lp queue to the printer, sending mail messages that have been queued, and carrying out uucp activities. You need only start these processes once when you bring up the system; then, they run themselves automatically.

To start these processes, you can either execute them manually from a command line or you can place them in a start-up file. For example, update automatically updates your disks every thirty seconds as long as the system is running. Your first choice is to start this program as a background process, as follows:

```
# /etc/update &
# _
```

195

Your other choice is to place this command line in a file called /etc/rc, which is the system start-up file. (It's similar to the start-up file for your own shell, .profile or .login.) The system start-up file lists all the commands that you want started when you boot the system.

> ▶ The /etc/rc file in UNIX is like the AUTOEXEC.BAT file in DOS.

The System Timer   *cron*

A command called cron acts as the UNIX system timer, starting processes at times that you designate. It's fairly similar to the timer on a video cassette recorder (VCR). The key to using the command is entering the desired information into a file called /usr/lib/crontab, which accepts requests for processing 24 hours a day, seven days a week.

Each line in /usr/lib/crontab contains a starting time (or times) and a command. After you set up /usr/lib/crontab and start cron, all of the listed commands are automatically started at the designated times. You must enter these times in five fields (minute, hour, day of month, month, and day of week), using numeric values. The timer uses a 24-hour clock, with the following values allowed in each field:

Minute	Hour	Day of Month	Month	Day of Week
0-59	0-23	1-31	1-12	0-6

The counting of hours on a 24-hour clock begins at midnight, so that 03 means 3:00 A.M., while 15 means 3:00 P.M. The days of the week begin at zero on Sunday; in other words, 0 means Sunday, 1 means Monday, 2 means Tuesday, and so on. You can use an asterisk (*) in any of these fields to mean all times. For example, an asterisk (*) in the day-of-week field would mean "every day."

You can separate fields from each other with either blank spaces or tabs. You can place a comment in the file by preceding it with a number sign (#). The following line in /usr/lib/crontab displays the contents of a file called /etc/reminder on the screen of terminal 00 every weekday morning at 11:00 A.M.:

```
0 11 * * 1-5   cat /etc/reminder > /dev/tty00
```

In the preceding example, the first two numbers indicate the time of day (0 11 means 11:00 A.M.), the two asterisks indicate "every day of every month, and the numbers 1-5 mean "Monday through Friday."

Another Look at Permissions

Using Symbolic Notation

In Chapter 2, you learned how to change file permissions with the chmod command. For example, you could add execute permission to a file called `send` (make `send` executable) with the following command line:

```
$ chmod u+x send
$ _
```

You also learned how to read permissions by executing the `ls -l` command, as follows:

```
$ ls -l send
-rwxr-x---  1  paul         92  Mar 23  09:17  send
$ _
```

Using Numeric Notation

The line displayed by the previous `ls -l` command illustrates the use of symbolic notation. As a system administrator, you should also be aware of numeric notation. Here is how the permissions just shown would translate from symbolic to numeric notation:

197

Owner	Group	Others	
r w x	r - x	- - -	Permission string
1 1 1	1 0 1	0 0 0	Binary equivalent
7	5	0	Octal equivalent

As illustrated above, each letter translates into a binary 1 (permission granted), while each hyphen (–) translates into binary 0 (permission denied). Then the octal equivalent of the binary translation is a three-digit number that means the same as the permission string. In the previous example, 750 is the same as rwxr-x---.

The `chmod` command accepts either symbolic or numeric notation. In other words, the following command line would be equivalent to the command `chmod u+x send`:

```
$ chmod 750 send
$ _
```

Making Numeric Conversions

In the octal numbering system (base 8), three binary digits (base 2) become one octal digit. Here is a conversion table:

Binary	Octal
0 0 0	0
0 0 1	1
0 1 0	2
0 1 1	3
1 0 0	4
1 0 1	5
1 1 0	6
1 1 1	7

198

To simplify conversion, think of the three binary digits in a permission string as being worth 4, 2, and 1 respectively. For example:

r	w	x	
1	1	1	Binary equivalent
4	2	1	Value of each binary digit

$$4 + 2 + 1 = 7 \quad \text{Octal equivalent}$$

r, w, x — Symbolic permission string

Here are a few examples of equivalent permissions:

```
r-- --- ---
100 000 000      400

rw- r-- r--
110 100 100      644

rwx r-x r--
111 101 100      754

rwx rwx rwx
111 111 111      777
```

As you can see, the lowest permission possible for most users is 400, while the highest is 777.

▶ The following table will let you quickly "build" the correct octal number. Merely add the numbers that correspond to the permissions you want to grant.

400 = owner read	040 = group read	004 = others read
200 = owner write	020 = group write	002 = others write
100 = owner execute	010 = group execute	001 = others execute

Thus, the permissions `rwxr-x---` translate as 400 + 200 + 100 + 40 + 10 = 750.

199

Shutting the System Down

The Shutdown Script   */etc/shutdown*

Many systems run around the clock. However, if you should ever have to shut down your system, all you have to do is run the shell script that is stored in directory `/etc` in a file called `shutdown`. The command line is as follows:

```
# shutdown
```

The details of this script vary from one installation to another. However, when you activate this script, it will perform the following operations for you:

Make sure that the person running this script is in fact logged in as root

Determine whether or not any other users are still active on the system

Notify such users of the shutdown with the `wall` (write all) command

Stop daemons such as process accounting, error-logging, and the `lp` spooler

Complete all pending disk updates with the `sync` command

Unmount all devices with the `umount` (unmount) command

Terminate multiuser mode and return to single-user mode with the `init s` command

Unfamiliar Terms

Unfortunately, we haven't yet discussed all the terms and commands used in the previous list of shutdown tasks. Let's discuss those terms now.

Process accounting refers to a set of programs that monitor processes on the system. Information compiled by these programs can be used to bill users for their time.

The `sync` command is used to bring disk files up to date by writing to disk any information still in memory. The system works on processes in memory, making changes to files, but often defers the task of writing the changes to disk. The `sync` command forces the system to save all changes on disk, and thereby synchronizes the data in memory with the data on disk.

In DOS, you have to refer to each disk drive by name. For example, to copy files from drive C to drive A, you would enter the following command:

```
C:\> copy *.* a:
```

In UNIX, you are never aware of specific disk drives because they are all *mounted* on the file system. The file system unites all devices as one seamless whole. You simply write to a directory, without ever having to know which disk contains the directory.

Before you shut down the system, you must be sure that all mounted devices are unmounted.

Finally, when a UNIX system is first booted, it begins operation in single-user mode. In this mode, there is only one user, the super user. Single-user mode is required for performing system maintenance and for shutting down the system.

What You've Learned

This chapter discussed some of the basic tasks of system administration. A system administrator is responsible for all the day-to-day tasks that keep the system running smoothly.

The system administrator logs in as root and enters commands from a special shell prompt (#). The directory for system administration is called /etc.

A system administrator can reach users of the system by using the mail command, the wall command, the news command, or the /etc/motd file. To set up a new user account, add a line to the system password file, add a line to the system group file (if necessary), create a home directory, and create a start-up file in the new directory. The who command allows you to find out who is logged in.

The cpio command is probably the best of the UNIX commands for backing up files. The command has three keys: copying out (–o), copying in (–i), and passing (–p) files. You can pipe filenames to cpio from either ls or find.

201

You set the basic characteristics of a terminal with the stty command. To make sure that you can use a terminal for vi, your terminal name must be an entry in /etc/termcap (or /usr/lib/terminfo/*/*) and you must set the shell variable TERM to the entry selected. (In the Bourne shell, you also have to export TERM.)

A process that runs itself automatically in the background is called a *daemon*. You can set other processes on the system timer by entering a line in /usr/lib/crontab and executing /etc/cron. Each line in /usr/lib/crontab includes a time and a command line.

As a system administrator, you need to be familiar with numeric notation for file permissions. You can translate from the symbolic notation by converting permissions first to binary, then to octal notation.

You can shut down the system by executing a shell script called /etc/shutdown.

Chapter 8 Quiz

1. What is the system administrator's login name?
2. What is the command for logging in as system administrator when you're already logged in as an ordinary user?
3. What is the name of the system administrator's directory?
4. What is the name of the file that identifies users who are authorized to use the system?
5. You suspect that an unauthorized user has just logged into the system. What command do you use to find out who is currently logged in?
6. What is the name of the directory that contains the names of the system's device files (such as disk and tape drives)?
7. What is the name of the file that contains information for the system timer?
8. What is the command for changing file permissions?

Write a command line to accomplish each of the following tasks:

9. Back up files from the current directory (without subdirectories) to a tape drive (/dev/rmt/3) with blocking?
10. Back up files from the current directory (without subdirectories) to a disk drive (/dev/rdsk/c0d1s0)?
11. Restore the files backed up in Exercise 7? Assume you are now in the target directory.
12. Restore the files backed up in Exercise 8? Assume you are now in the target directory.
13. Copy the files in the current directory (/usr/willy/work) to a directory called /usr/willy/hold? (Display the name of each file being copied.)
14. Change the speed of your terminal to 1200 bits per second.
15. Change your terminal's erase character to Ctrl-H and change its kill character to Ctrl-E.
16. Make sure that all corrections on each command line are processed before the host computer receives them from your terminal.

Other questions:

17. What is the name of the original file that contains descriptions of terminals?
18. What is the name of the directory that will eventually replace the file named in Exercise 17?
19. What is the name of the shell variable that identifies your terminal type, as described in the file named in Exercise 17 (or the directory named in Exercise 18)?
20. Suppose your terminal type is `wyse50`. How would you make this known to your system if you're using the Bourne shell?
21. How would you do Exercise 20 if you were using the C shell?
22. Referring to Exercises 20 and 21, name the file in which you would place each statement.
23. To display the contents of a file called `/usr/paul/news` on terminal number 7 every Friday morning at 9:30 A.M., what would you enter in `/usr/lib/crontab`?
24. Write a command line in numeric notation that is equivalent to the following:

```
$ chmod u=rwx,g=r-x,o=r-x repeat
```

203

absolute pathname A pathname that explicitly identifies all directories from the root directory to an individual file. For example, pathname `/usr/albert/info/test` refers to a file named `test` in directory `info`, which belongs to directory `albert`, which belongs to directory `usr`, which belongs to the root directory `/`.

access As a noun, the ability to read, write, or execute files within a UNIX system. As a verb, to use that ability. Access to files in a UNIX file system is controlled by a set of permissions established by the system administrator. As superuser, the system administrator has unlimited access within the system.

account A home directory and a set of access privileges assigned to a user to allow that user to carry out tasks in a UNIX system. Each new user is typically assigned a login name and a password, which allow the user to log in and begin using the resources of the system.

address In computer usage in general, the location at which something is stored in a computer system. Text, data, and computer programs are stored in memory and on disk at addresses, which are usually expressed as numeric values.

alias An alternate name, or abbreviation, used in place of a command or a sequence of commands in the C shell and the Korn shell.

append To place after, or at the end, of a character, a line, or a file. In the vi editor, certain commands let you append text in a document. In the Bourne and C shells, the symbol >> allows you to append output to an existing file (or create a new file if the file does not yet exist).

append mode In vi, the mode that allows you to type new text after existing text in a file; terminate this mode by pressing Esc.

argument On a command line, a name or code that is included with a command to modify the output of the command. For example, the command line ls –l has a single argument (–l). The shell identifies the command name with the notation $0, the first argument with $1, the second argument with $2, and so on.

ASCII Acronym for American Standard Code for Information Interchange. A coding scheme for characters that appear on most keyboards, along with a set of control codes for operating terminals and printers. UNIX, DOS, and other operating systems for smaller computer systems use ASCII characters for input, output, and control. In Europe, the set of 128 7-bit codes is known as the ISO (International Standards Organization) character set. To accommodate accented characters in Europe and oriental character sets in Asia, UNIX is moving toward expanding the original 7-bit set into 8-bit extensions, which include 256 characters.

206

assign To give a value to a variable in a programming or configuration statement. For example, in the Bourne shell statement TERM=vt100, you assign the value vt100 to the environmental variable TERM, which identifies your terminal type (VT100) to the UNIX system.

background Processing that a system performs without requiring interaction with the user. In UNIX, append an ampersand (&) to the command line to request background processing.

background process A process that runs without interacting with a terminal. Because each user in a UNIX system is allowed to have a number of background processes running simultaneously, UNIX is called a *multitasking* system.

backslash A character (\) that is used in shell statements to *quote* another character (that is, to remove its special meaning to the shell). For example, if you want to use a dollar sign as a dollar sign, rather than as a symbol for end of line, enter \$.

backup A copy of a file (or a group of files) that is stored off-line in the event that a computer system fails, losing or damaging the original file or files.

basename The name of a file minus any extension that may be included in the full name. For example, if the full name of the source file for a C program is `combine.c`, its basename is `combine`.

batch processing The opposite of *interactive processing*; work that is collected at a peripheral site, then forwarded to a central computer at the end of a fixed period. Such work may be forwarded at the end of each hour, each day, or each week.

baud rate See *data rate*.

Berkeley UNIX The versions of UNIX that were first developed at the University of California in Berkeley in the mid-1970s. Many features originally part of Berkeley UNIX, such as the `vi` editor and the C shell, have since been incorporated into XENIX and AT&T UNIX.

bin A directory that contains executable programs, the majority of which are stored in binary files. Most programs are found in directories `/bin` and `/usr/bin`; however, users often keep additional programs in private `bin` directories, such as `/usr/charles/bin`.

bit Acronym for *bi*nary digi*t*, the basic atomic unit of a digital computer. There are eight bits in each *byte*, which contains one character.

block A set of data (typically 256, 512, or 1,024 bytes) that is stored as a unit on a tape or disk.

bold In printing, a font style that uses heavier strokes than the standard font (which is called *roman*).

boot To begin the operation of a computer system, using a bootstrap program that copies the operating system from disk to memory. In UNIX, the booting process includes one phase to initiate single-user operation and another phase to carry out a transition from single-user to multiple-user operation. A shell script called `/etc/rc` aids in the booting process by running many programs and processes automatically.

Bourne shell The original command processor for the UNIX system, which is still the most widely used. The Bourne shell lacks the more sophisticated features of the C shell and the Korn shell, but it runs faster.

braces A pair of symbols ({ and }) that are used to group items in a statement. In the Bourne shell, braces surround commands that are to be executed together; in the C shell, braces indicate variable names and cause a list of items to be expanded.

brackets A pair of symbols ([and]) that are used to group items in a statement. In all shells and in editors, square brackets are used to identify a set of characters.

BSD Berkeley Software Distribution, used to identify various versions of Berkeley UNIX, such as BSD 4.2 and BSD 4.3.

buffer In computer technology in general, an area in memory where information is stored temporarily, usually for an intermediary step in a process. When you use a text editor, you first enter the text in a buffer, and then you store it in a disk file.

bug A hardware or software error. According to tradition, the term originated when an early computer failure was found to be the result of a dead insect.

bus An internal communication network in a computer system. A typical system includes an address bus, a data bus, and a control bus. The width of the address bus determines the amount of memory that can be addressed by the system.

byte A unit of eight bits, which contains a single character of text. The capacity of memory and disks is measured in bytes, kilobytes, and megabytes.

carriage return A character, abbreviated as CR, that is used in most ASCII systems to terminate a line of text. The key that generates the character, Ctrl-M, is labeled either *Enter* or *Return* on most keyboards. In UNIX, newline (NL) is used instead of carriage return (CR) to terminate lines.

case The capitalization or non-capitalization of a character. Capitalized characters are called uppercase; non-capitalized characters are called lowercase. In MS-DOS, case is ignored in filenames; in UNIX, case is considered.

character The basic unit of textprocessing, which can be any of the following: a letter of the alphabet, a number, a symbol, a blank space, or a control character. Most control characters are typed by holding down the Ctrl (control) key and pressing another key on the keyboard.

child process A process spawned from another process. The original process is called the *parent*, and the new process is called the *child*. To create a new process, the UNIX system duplicates an existing process and then changes the recently created duplicate to the process desired. This is known as *forking*.

chip A tiny piece of semiconductor material, usually silicon, onto which have been etched a set of electronic circuits. A hundred or more chips can be sliced from each silicon wafer, which is two or three inches in diameter. Because each chip is housed in a package with metallic leads, people often refer to the entire package as a chip. Dozens of chips can be plugged into a circuit board, and a set of circuit boards form a computer system.

C language A computer programming language that combines the ease of use of a high-level language with the system-control features of a low-level language. About 90 percent of the UNIX system is written in C. During the 1970s, UNIX and C were closely related, but now C has become a separate tool in its own right and is used widely outside UNIX.

209

command A request to have something accomplished by a computer system using a computer program. The program can be as simple as `date`, which merely displays the date and time, or as complex as `vi`, which offers a sophisticated set of editing tools.

command line A line of input, usually from a keyboard, that includes at least one command, along with any accompanying arguments and connectors. Commands can be grouped together on a command line or connected by a pipe. In addition, the input and output of commands can be redirected. In the following example, the `ls` command, modified by the `-l` argument, is piped to the `pg` command:

```
$ ls -l ¦ pg
```

command name A name for a program that you can type at your keyboard to have the program executed. The name of the command can usually be followed by arguments on a command line.

command processor A program that interprets command lines and provides for carrying out the tasks requested in command lines. In the UNIX system, the command processor is also known as the *shell*. There are three command processors used on UNIX systems: the Bourne shell, the C shell, and the Korn shell. See also *Bourne shell, C shell,* and *Korn shell.*

communication speed See *data rate*.

compile To translate the high-level symbolic notation used in a computer program into the low-level coding required to run the program on the computer.

compiler A computer program that translates high-level programs, called source files, into low-level programs, called object files.

computer An electronic machine that can perform a variety of high-speed tasks under the direction of a *program* or a set of programs. A program that handles the basic functioning of the computer is called an operating system; a program that is used to carry out a specific task for a user is called an application program. UNIX is an example of an operating system.

concatenate To join two or more files or segments of text to form a single unit. The `cat` command, which is an abbreviation of this word, concatenates files.

210

configure To adjust the hardware or software components of a system to certain specifications. A particular arrangement of devices or programs is called a *configuration*.

console A computer system's main terminal, from which system administration is performed. Recent releases of UNIX allow any terminal to be designated as the console, which is identified by device file `/dev/console`.

constant An assigned value that remains unchanged, as opposed to a *variable*.

control character A character, usually generated by holding down the Ctrl key and pressing another key, that is used to control the operation of the terminal or the printer. For example, Ctrl-I causes an advance to the next tab stop on terminals and printers that support this feature. A key control character in the UNIX system is Ctrl-D, which indicates end of file (and end of session).

controller A machine that handles the flow of data to and from a peripheral device, such as a disk or tape drive.

cooked mode A mode in which input is accepted command line by command line rather than character by character. Cooked mode, the default for the UNIX system, is the opposite of *raw mode*.

core An obsolete term for computer memory.

core dump A recording of the contents of computer memory at the moment when an error occurred. Unfortunately for ordinary users, core dumps are left in working directories in ordinary files named `core`. The contents of these files are of value only to those who are familiar with the internal workings of the UNIX system.

cpio A UNIX program that is used to copy files in one of three different ways: from a working directory to a backup device, from a backup device to a working directory, or from one directory to another.

crash A major hardware or software failure, which interrupts the functioning of a computer system.

cron A UNIX daemon that periodically checks the contents of a file called `/usr/lib/crontab` and carries out any tasks due to be performed.

crontab A short name for file `/usr/lib/crontab`, which contains a list of UNIX commands to be performed at specific times. A system administrator can use `crontab` as an automatic timer to trigger the initiation of important jobs.

211

CRT Abbreviation for cathode-ray tube, which provides the screen display for most terminals.

C shell The command processor that was designed at the University of California by William N. Joy and others. This command processor allows you to retrieve previous command lines (which are called *events*) and re-execute them, either with or without modification.

cursor The symbol that appears on your video screen to indicate the location of the next character that you type from your keyboard.

daemon A program that, once activated, starts itself and carries out a specific task. The UNIX system uses daemons extensively to handle jobs that have been queued, such as printing, mail, and communication.

data Information that is to be, or has been, processed by a computer. Strictly speaking, *data* is the plural of *datum*, but it is often used collectively as if it were singular.

data rate In all forms of communication, the rate at which data is sent or received, measured in bits per second. Also referred to as *communication speed, bit rate,* and *baud rate.*

debug To rid hardware or software of errors, or bugs.

decimal With reference to numbers, base ten.

default A selection or value that is provided by computer hardware or software when you don't make an explicit choice.

delete To remove a segment of text, a file, or a directory. The vi editor has several commands, including x and d, to delete text. The UNIX rm command is used to delete a file; the rmdir command is used to delete a directory.

device In computer usage in general, any piece of equipment that is connected directly to a computer, such as a terminal, printer, modem, disk drive, or tape drive. Also called a *peripheral device*, an *input/output device*, or an *I/O device*. In UNIX, a file system becomes a logical device, eliminating the need to refer to disk drives by name.

device file A file that represents a physical device that is mounted on a UNIX system. All device files, also known as *special files*, are stored in directory /dev.

directory In operating systems in general, a file that contains the names of other files. UNIX has a primal directory that is called *root* (represented by /), along with subdirectories organized in a hierarchy. When you log into a UNIX system, you start in your home directory. You can change to another directory with the cd command, display the name of the current directory with the pwd command, create a directory with the mkdir command, display the contents of a directory with the ls command, and remove a directory with the rmdir command. You can use a single dot (.) to represent the current directory and a pair of dots (..) to refer to the parent directory.

disk A mass storage medium that employs a magnetic coating on a round, flat substance that holds electrical charges. If the underlying substance (called the *substrate*) is plastic, it is a floppy disk, or a diskette; if the substrate is metallic, it is a hard disk.

document Another term for a file that contains text.

DOS An operating system developed for microcomputers in the early 1980s (the version that runs on the IBM Personal Computer is called PC DOS). Originally patterned after CP/M, more recent versions of MS-DOS have been heavily influenced by UNIX concepts.

drive A mechanical device that spins a storage medium (disk or tape), reads data from it, and writes data to it.

driver A program that handles the details of interface between a computer and a peripheral device.

echo To repeat on the screen characters that are entered at the keyboard. You can use the `echo` command to explicitly display a string of characters.

ed The original UNIX text editor that preceded `vi`. The `ed` program is a primitive line editor that lacks the full-screen capabilities of `vi`.

edit To make changes to a file, such as moving, copying, inserting, and deleting text.

editor A program that is used to make changes to a file. The two programs used most often on UNIX systems are the `ed` line editor and the full-screen `vi` visual interpreter. The programmable `emacs` editor is also used at many UNIX installations.

environment A set of shell variables and their assigned values provided for each process that is called. The default environment for your terminal is stored in your home directory in a file called either `.profile` (Bourne shell) or `.login` (C shell). You can modify the environment by reassigning shell variables.

213

eqn A preprocessor for `troff` that lets you format mathematical expressions. The corresponding preprocessor for `nroff` is called `neqn`.

erase character The character that is used to erase the character just typed on a command line—usually either the number symbol (#) or backspace (Ctrl-H).

Esc The escape key, which is used in `vi` to leave text-entry mode and return to command mode.

ex An enhanced version of the `ed` line editor. The `vi` editor is the visual interpreter of `ex`.

execute To run a program. On a `chmod` command line, you can add or remove permission to execute a file using the x symbol. You must have execute permission for a directory to be able to change to that directory or to be able to include that directory's name in a pathname given on a command line.

expression A representation of a number or text that can vary, depending on how individual values are interpreted. Expressions are often used to match text in a file or match filenames in a directory. An example of an expression is `memo.*`, which may be used to match `memo.402`, `memo.TKL`, `memo.old`, and so on.

extension That part of a filename that follows a period (also known as a *suffix*). For example, each source file for a C program has an extension of .c.

field In text-processing, a segment of a line of text that may be named and processed by a program. The sort program can use fields when it sorts lines in a file. In UNIX, fields are usually separated by spaces or tabs.

field separator A character, also called a *delimiter*, that is used to separate one field from another. The default field separator for many programs, such as sort, is a blank space (or a tab).

file A collection of characters that has a name and may contain text, a program, data, the names of other files, or information about a device. A file that contains the names of other files is called a *directory*; a file that contains information about a device is called a *device file* (or *special file*); and a file that begins with a period is called an *invisible file* (because the ls command without an argument won't display it).

214

filename The name given to a file, which must be unique within any given directory. In UNIX, you can use as many as 14 characters in a filename, including hyphens, periods, and plus signs.

file system A set of files on a disk, together with the information required to manage the files. The directories within a UNIX file system form a hierarchy.

file type A description of the function of a file. These types include ordinary files, directories, and special files, which represent devices in the system.

filter A program that takes a set of data (usually in a file) as input, processes the data, and makes the processed data its output. Some examples of filters include grep, sort, awk, and sed.

foreground A conceptual location in a computer system where interaction takes place between a user and a process initiated by the user; the opposite of *background*.

format To prepare a document for printing by filling and aligning lines of text, by marking bold and underlining, and by making other enhancements to a printed page.

full duplex A communication mode that allows data to flow in both directions simultaneously.

global From the beginning of a file to the end. This term is often used to describe an operation such as a search; the opposite of *local*.

grep A program that allows you to search for occurrences of text in a file (or in a group of files).

group A collection of users on a UNIX system who have something in common and share a group identifier. All those working on a particular project or all members of a certain organization may belong to a group. Group identifiers are listed in the `/etc/passwd` file.

half-duplex A communication mode that allows data to flow in only one direction at a time.

hardware The electronic components of a computer system, as opposed to *software*, the programs that run on the system.

hardwired terminal A terminal that is connected to a host computer via a dedicated line (that is, a line that is not shared with any other terminal).

215

hexadecimal With reference to numbers, base sixteen. To express hexadecimal numbers, the following digits are used: 0, 1, 2, 3, 4, 5, 6, 7, 8, 9, A, B, C, D, E, F. For example, the decimal number 26 would be represented in hexadecimal notation as 1A.

high-level language A computer language that can be used on many different computer systems. By contrast, a *low-level language* refers to specific hardware locations and is inseparable from a specific hardware architecture. Another name for low-level language is *assembly language*.

history In the C shell and the Korn shell, a list of command lines (or events) previously executed by a user.

home directory The directory that a user enters after logging into a UNIX system; also called the *login directory*.

host A central computer, also known as a *host computer*, which provides processing for terminals and other peripheral devices (and, in some instances, other computers).

indent To offset text from the margin. You can indent either the first line of a paragraph or all lines.

input Data entered into a computer system to be processed by a program.

insert mode In `vi`, the mode that allows you to type new text in front of existing text in a file; terminate this mode by pressing Esc.

install To connect a piece of hardware to a computer system; to place the program files of a piece of software in a directory, where they can be executed.

interactive processing Performance of tasks on a computer system that involves continual exchange of information between the computer and a user; the opposite of *batch processing*.

I/O Abbreviation for input/output: the transfer of data between a computer and its peripheral equipment, or devices.

italic In printing, a font style that uses slanted strokes and rounded corners.

justify In text-formatting, to align text flush left or flush right (or both) against a margin.

kernel The program that interacts between a UNIX system and computer hardware. The kernel occupies approximately 10% of the UNIX system.

kill character The key that you use to erase a command line, often either the at sign (@) or Ctrl-U.

Korn shell The most recent command processor, named after David G. Korn, which combines the advantages of the earlier Bourne shell and C shell.

laser printer A printer that employs the technology of a photocopier and is capable of printing text (in varied fonts) and graphics together on the same page.

link Attachment of an existing file to a directory (usually a different directory) that allows file-sharing. You can use the `ln` command to form a new link.

local Restricted to only part of a file; the opposite of *global*.

login name The name by which a user logs into a UNIX system; any files owned by the user are identified by this name.

logout Termination of a UNIX session. Merely turning off your terminal isn't always enough; sometimes you must end a session by logging out.

low-level language A computer language that deals with hardware registers by name; also known as *assembly language*. A program written in a low-level language can be used only on a computer system that uses one type of main processor (or possibly a member of a family of processors). Assembly language, which uses symbolic addressing, is one step away from machine language.

macro A command that incorporates a set of other commands. You custom design a command, called a macro, from existing commands. Both the `vi` editor and the `nroff/troff` formatters use macros. The `mm` macro package described in this book is an example of a large collection of `nroff/troff` macros.

magnetic tape A storage medium that allows you to archive a large amount of data relatively inexpensively. Files stored on magnetic tape, unlike those stored on disk, cannot be retrieved by random access. You can back up files to magnetic tape using several different programs, such as `dd`, `tar`, and `cpio`. The `cpio` program is described in this book in detail.

mainframe The largest and most powerful type of computer system that is widely used. A mainframe typically occupies many cabinets and fills an entire room. Amdahl's UTS is a UNIX-derived operating system that runs on mainframes.

man A program that lets you display pages from the UNIX reference manual. For example, if you want detailed information about the `who` command, you enter `man who` at the shell prompt. (The `man` program may or may not be available at your particular UNIX site.)

-man An `nroff/troff` macro package that is specifically designed to handle pages from the UNIX reference manual.

mass storage device A piece of equipment, such as a disk or tape drive, that stores large amounts of data relatively inexpensively. Although these devices cost less than the main memory in a computer system, they are much slower to access. The UNIX system is designed to be stored on disk, while those files needed at a particular moment are copied to memory for processing. Mass storage devices are also used for daily and weekly backups.

-me An `nroff/troff` macro package, developed for Berkeley UNIX systems, that formats documents.

medium A disk, tape, or other object on which information is actually stored. Most media used today employ a metallic substance, such as iron oxide, to capture magnetic charges. However, a newer technology involving plastic discs and optical scanning (CD-ROM) will eventually supercede today's magnetic methods.

memory The electronic work area of a computer where actual processing takes place. Today's state-of-the-art desktop computer has at least one megabyte of memory. During the first twenty years or so of the computer age, memory was constructed using tiny mag-

217

netic rings called *cores* and was referred to as *core memory*. This terminology has survived in the UNIX system; a recording of memory contents at the moment of a failure is still called a *core dump*.

metacharacter A character that is used to carry a special meaning, such as a caret (∧, beginning of line), a dollar sign ($, end of line), or an asterisk (*, match any character). To use one of these characters without special meaning, you must either precede it with a backslash (\) or enclose it within quotation marks. Bypassing the special meaning of a metacharacter is called *escaping* or *quoting* the character.

microcomputer A small desktop computer, also called a personal computer, that is usually used by one person at a time.

microprocessor A main processor (or CPU, central processing unit) that is usually contained on a single chip.

minicomputer An intermediate-size computer, typically about the size of a refrigerator. The UNIX system was originally developed in the late 1960s and early 1970s on a minicomputer, the PDP-7 of Digital Equipment Corporation.

-mm An `nroff/troff` macro package for formatting manuscripts; the standard macro package of UNIX System V. It is the most extensive macro package available.

modem Abbreviation for modulator/demodulator, a device that translates digital codes into tones (that is, modulates them) and translates tones into digital codes (that is, demodulates them). The purpose of a modem is to allow you to send information from a digital computer system across telephone lines to another computer system. In the twenty-first century, when analog telephone lines are replaced with optical fiber lines capable of carrying audio, data, and video signals, there will no longer be a need for modems.

mount To connect a device to the UNIX system and thereby integrate it into the system.

-ms An `nroff/troff` macro package for formatting manuscripts; the standard macro package for the UNIX system before System V.

Multics The predecessor of the UNIX system; an experimental operating system developed by MIT and Bell Laboratories in the 1960s. The UNIX system derived much of its technology (and its name) from Multics.

multiplex To interleave signals or data from different sources. The UNIX system employs multiplexing of memory.

multitasking Running more than one process at once by relying on time-sharing techniques.

multiuser Supporting more than one user. UNIX is a multiuser, multitasking operating system.

network A system of hardware and software that connects a group of computers and allows them to transmit information back and forth to each other. Networks are usually classed as either local-area networks (LAN) or wide-area networks (WAN).

neqn An `nroff` preprocessor that lets you format mathematical expressions for character printers. (The corresponding `troff` pre-processor is called `eqn`.)

nroff The UNIX text formatting program that handles text that is to be printed on character printers. The `troff` program handles text to be printed on laser printers and phototypesetters. Otherwise, the two programs are nearly identical.

219

octal With reference to numbers, base 8. The octal digits are 0, 1, 2, 3, 4, 5, 6, and 7.

operating system A program that manages the details of operating a computer system. These details include managing memory, keeping track of directories and files, scheduling processes, and handling input/output operations. Application programs rely on the operating system to perform tasks.

option An argument on a command line, usually preceded by a minus sign, that modifies the functioning of the command—also known as a *flag* or a *switch*. For example, the `-x` option on the command line `vi -x` allows the `vi` editor to read an encrypted file.

ordinary file The most common type of file in a UNIX file system; it contains text, programs, or data. When you display a list of files with the command `ls -l`, ordinary files are identified by hyphens (`-`).

output Data that has been processed by a computer program.

owner The user who creates a file and therefore has privileged access to it.

parent directory The directory above the current directory. In the hierarchy of a UNIX file system, every directory except root has a parent. You can refer to the parent directory using the double dot notation (..).

password A personal identifier used to validate a user's authorization to log into a UNIX system. A password may consist of one to fourteen characters, but an effective password should be at least six characters long. It should contain a combination of upper- and lowercase letters, numbers, and symbols that you can easily memorize. However, it should not contain a sequence that is easy to guess, such as the name of a relative, spouse, or pet, your telephone number, or your license number.

password file A file, /etc/passwd, that contains basic information about each user authorized to log into a given UNIX system. For each user, the file contains a line that gives the user's login name, password, user identifier, group identifier (if any), home directory, and login program.

pathname A sequence of directory names that indicates the location of a file in a UNIX file system. A *relative pathname* gives the location relative to the current directory; an *absolute pathname* gives the location with respect to the root directory. Each directory name is separated from the next name lower in the hierarchy by a slash (/), while the root directory is denoted by a slash (/) and nothing more. Suppose you are currently in directory /usr/albert/plans and want to refer to another directory under albert called letters. The absolute pathname would be /usr/albert/letters (the same from any directory); the relative pathname would be ../letters.

peripheral device See *device*.

personal computer A computer intended for use by one person; also called a *microcomputer*. The most widely used personal computers today are the IBM Personal Computer (along with its derivatives and compatibles) and the Apple Macintosh. As noted early in this book, a personal computer can be used as a terminal in a UNIX system. The most powerful personal computers, such as those that are based on the 80386 microprocessor, are capable of running UNIX itself.

phototypesetter An expensive, high-quality, high-resolution printer that produces printed output for professional work. Like a much lower-resolution laser printer, a phototypesetter is capable of generating a variety of typefaces in different sizes. In UNIX, the `troff` program formats text that is intended for laser printers and phototypesetters.

pica A unit of measure in typography (1/6 of an inch), commonly used to indicate the length of a line of type. For example, a column that is three and a half inches wide is 21 picas wide. Picas are often combined with *points* for more precise measurements. For example, you could express 7/12 of an inch as 3,06 (3 picas and 6 points). See also *point*.

pid See *process identification number.*

pipe A programming device that lets you use the output of one process as the input of another. You must use a vertical bar (¦) between two command invocations to indicate piping. For example, to display the contents of the current directory one screenful at a time, you can pipe the `ls -l` command through the `pg` command, as follows:

221

```
$ ls -l ¦ pg
```

The result of this command line is that the `pg` command uses the file display generated by `ls -l` as its input. The output is the file display in 24-line segments that will fit on your screen.

pipeline A sequence of commands connected by pipes. For example, to display the lines of a file called `entries` in alphabetical order, you could construct the following command line:

```
$ cat entries ¦ sort ¦ pg
```

When you execute this command line, the `cat` command retrieves the file, the `sort` command arranges the lines in order, and the `pg` command displays the result in 24-line segments.

point A unit of measure in typography (1/72 of an inch), used to indicate the size of a typeface. Most ordinary text is set in 10, 11, or 12 points; headings are usually set in approximately 12 to 24 points; and chapter headings are generally 24 points or larger. There are 12 points in a *pica*, and the two units are often combined in typographic measurements. For example, you could express a quarter of an inch as 1,06 (1 pica and 6 points).

port To modify software so that it will operate in a different environment. For example, a programmer could modify a DOS program to allow it to run under UNIX, or modify a UNIX system designed for a minicomputer so that it will run on a microcomputer.

A *port* is also an input or output data path on a microcomputer (called a *channel* on a mainframe).

portable Pertaining to software that can be ported, or modified to run in another environment. UNIX is an example of a portable system. Because all the programming that is hardware-specific is restricted to the *kernel*, a programmer can port UNIX to a new computer system by changing only the kernel (about 10 to 15% of the total UNIX code).

preprocessor A program that manipulates data before the primary processing program goes to work. Examples are the `eqn` and `tbl` programs that handle equations and tables before `troff` performs general-purpose formatting on a text file.

process The computer activity that takes place while a command is being executed. In the UNIX system, there can be many processes that represent different invocations of the same program. The kernel assigns a unique process identification number (pid) to each process active in the system.

process identification number Usually abbreviated pid, a number that the kernel assigns to a process active in a UNIX system. The pid is especially important for background processes, because you must know the number to terminate the process. If you start a background process, you can determine the pid in two ways: (1) note the number when the shell displays it on the screen; (2) display it by using the `ps` command.

program A sequence of instructions to a computer system, which directs the operation of the system. The concept of a program is what distinguishes a computer from nearly every other type of machine. To operate a lawnmower or a bicycle, you manually direct the operation of the machine with your hands and feet. To operate a computer, you have to provide the machine with a detailed list of instructions, which the machine appears to perform on its own.

Programs are referred to collectively as *software* and are classed as either those that aid the computer in its basic functioning (operating systems) or those that are designed to carry out a specific task (application software). Application programs perform the work that people use computers for; an operating system carries out the administrative tasks that allow application programs to function smoothly.

222

When writing programs, programmers use a *programming language* to facilitate the job. Such a language lets the programmer work with a set of notational conventions that lend themselves to human usage. However, before the program can be used by the computer, it must be translated into a set of codes than lend themselves to machine operation. For a high-level language (such as FORTRAN, Pascal, or C), the process of translating the program is called *compiling*; for a low-level assembly language, the process is called *assembling* the program. A program that compiles other programs is called a *compiler*; a program that assembles other programs is called an *assembler*. Another type of high-level language (such as BASIC) is interpreted line-by-line by a program called an *interpreter*. Programs written in low-level languages run the fastest of all types of programs; programs written in interpreted languages run the slowest.

programming language See *program*.

prompt Text or symbols that appear on the screen to solicit input from a user. The most common prompt in the UNIX system is the one that informs you that the system is ready to accept a command line. The default for this prompt on most systems is a dollar sign ($) for the Bourne shell, a percent sign (%) for the C shell, and a pound sign (#) for the superuser.

pwd A UNIX command that displays the name of the current directory (*print working directory*).

queue A list of jobs awaiting execution (from the French word for "line"). Queues in a UNIX system are nearly always processed by *daemon*. See also *daemon*.

quoting Preventing special characters from being interpreted as special characters, often using quotation marks. To quote a string of characters, you can surround them with either double quotes ("*string*") or single quotes ('*string*')—single quotes are used more extensively. To quote a single character, precede it with a backslash (\). For example, to read a dollar sign as a dollar sign (rather than as a symbol for end-of-line), enter \$.

raw mode A mode in which characters entered into the UNIX system are read and interpreted one at a time. See also *cooked mode*.

real-time processing Processing by a computer system that takes place inside the computer while events related to the processing are taking place outside the computer. An example is the processing used to determine a missile's position during a missile launch; the processing must keep pace with external events. Earlier versions of UNIX were not suitable for real-time applications; however, efforts are under way to correct this deficiency in newer releases.

record In database applications, a complete set of information for one item. Each individual piece of information is contained in a *field*; a given number of fields form a record. Some files, such as /etc/passwd, /etc/group, and /usr/lib/crontab, contain one-line records; others, such as /etc/termcap and /usr/lib/terminfo/* contain multiple-line records.

redirection The act of either accepting input from a source other than the standard input (the keyboard) or sending output to a destination other than the standard output (the video screen). The symbols used are the less than sign (<) for redirection of input and the greater than sign (>) for redirection of output. For example, to send to Paul a message already typed and stored in a file called news, use the following command line:

```
$ mail paul < news
```

To store the contents of the current directory in a file called files, use the following command line:

```
$ ls -l > files
```

To append text to an existing file, you can use the double greater than sign (>>), as in the following example:

```
$ ls -l >> files
```

regular expression A set of symbols, including text and metacharacters, used to search for text. The most common components are the period (.), which matches one character; the asterisk (*), which matches any number of characters; and brackets ([*string*]), which list a set of characters to be matched.

relative pathname See *pathname*.

request An nroff/troff command. Most of these include a period, followed by two lowercase letters. Many requests also include a numeric argument, such as the page offset request, .po *n*

restore To retrieve data that has been previously backed up from a computer system. If your computer system fails, you might have to restore data to resume use of the system.

roman In typesetting, the normal font, which is neither bold nor italic.

root The primary directory in the UNIX system; the login name for the superuser. A system administrator who is just logging in can log in as superuser by typing `root`; one who is already logged in as an ordinary user can enter the `su` (substitute user) command. Either way, the next step is to enter the superuser password.

RS-232C A standard for serial communication that is used to connect computers, terminals, printers, and modems. The complete standard calls for 25 wires, but many configurations use as few as three (send, receive, and ground). A typical RS-232C connector is enclosed in a trapezoidal case about two inches wide and one-half inch high.

scrolling The act of shifting a screen display up or down one line at a time.

search path A list of directories in which a given user's commands may be found. Each time the user enters a command at the keyboard, the shell searches the list to find the command. You can execute only those commands that belong to the directories in your search path. The search path is usually found in the initialization file (`.profile` for the Bourne shell or `.login` for the C shell).

225

security Measures taken to keep intruders out of a computer system. The UNIX system uses login names and passwords to maintain security, and these provide a fairly good defense against unauthorized entry. However, sophisticated intruders have devised a number of clever schemes for bypassing ordinary UNIX security.

session One complete interaction between a user and the UNIX system, from login to logout. It is possible for a given user to carry on more than one session at a time using either windows or several different terminals.

shell A command processor for the UNIX system, which includes its own programming language. As command processor, the shell interprets command lines and arranges to have the requested tasks performed. As programming language, the shell supports variables, logical control, and conditional statements. The original command processor is called the Bourne shell; an enhanced version developed at the University of California is called the C shell; a more recent version that combines the features of both is called the Korn shell. The Bourne and Korn shells are named for their originators; the C shell is named after the C programming language, from which it borrows many features. The word "shell" conveys the sense of something that houses something else within it. You can think of the shell as a process that surrounds the kernel and conceals it from the ordinary user.

sleep Pertaining to a UNIX process, to suspend execution until some event takes place or for a specific period of time. Processes automatically sleep while waiting for results from peripherals. In addition, you can request a general suspension with the `sleep` command.

software A collective name for the programs that run on a computer system, as opposed to *hardware*, the electronic components.

sorting The process of rearranging a list of items in a prescribed order. The UNIX `sort` command lets you sort information in a variety of different ways.

226

special character A character used to form a *regular expression* for the purpose of carrying out a search; also called a *metacharacter*.

special file A file that represents a hardware device; also known as a *device file*.

standard input The expected source of input to a process (the keyboard is the default).

standard output The expected destination of output from a process (the video screen is the default).

string In computer usage in general, a sequence of characters.

su A UNIX command (substitute user) that allows a user to use a different login name. If you have more than one account on a UNIX system, you can change from one to the other with the `su` command. By issuing this command without an argument, a system administrator can change from ordinary user to superuser.

subdirectory A directory that is directly below another in the hierarchy of the UNIX file system. In a pathname, the slash (`/`) separates the name of each subdirectory from its parent. For example, `/usr/chet/files` is a subdirectory of `/usr/chet`.

superuser A term used to describe the system administrator as a user of a UNIX system, particularly the system administrator's freedom of access without regard to permissions.

sync A UNIX command that updates files by writing from memory to disk. You can think of this command as the one that synchronizes disk space with memory.

tab A control character (Ctrl-I) that causes either a cursor to advance to a predetermined horizontal location (terminal) or a printhead to advance (printer).

tape drive A machine that reads from and writes to magnetic tape. Because the data is stored sequentially on the tape, this kind of mass storage device is best suited for full system backups.

tar A UNIX program (tape archive) that lets you copy files to and from magnetic tape, using a variety of options. (In XENIX, the program is also used to copy to and from diskettes.)

tbl An `nroff/troff` preprocessor that lets you format tabular material.

tee A UNIX program that allows you to send text to a file and display the text on the screen simultaneously. As shown in the following example, the `tee` command is always preceded by a pipe symbol (¦):

227

```
$ ls -l ¦ tee files
```

The list of filenames is displayed on the screen and also stored in `files`. Now you can retrieve the information using `cat`, `pg`, or `more` or edit it using `vi`.

TeleType A type of terminal, in use until about the mid-1970s, that employed printing on a roll of paper rather than a video display. The prevalence of this type of terminal during the period when UNIX was being developed made the words terminal and teletype nearly synonymous in UNIX terminology. The abbreviation `tty` is used to this day to represent "terminal," even though teletype machines are now obsolete.

$TERM A shell variable that identifies the type of terminal you are using. The name assigned to this variable must be defined in the UNIX system's terminal definition file (`termcap` or `terminfo`).

termcap A file (pathname `/etc/termcap`) that describes the capabilities of each terminal that can be used on a given UNIX system. The `termcap` file (terminal capability) is gradually being superceded by a newer `terminfo` file in System V.

terminal An interactive device that enables you to use a computer system. Modern video terminals include a keyboard, a monitor, and possibly a microprocessor. The printing terminals of the 1960s included a keyboard and a printer.

terminfo A directory that contains descriptions of the functions of all the terminals that can be used on a UNIX system. The full pathname of the directory is `/usr/lib/terminfo`. This feature of UNIX System V is designed to replace `termcap` eventually.

text Written material that has been generated by a computer system. Memos, letters, reports, articles, and books all consist of text. Within a computer system, text is made up of codes that represent letters, numbers, symbols, punctuation, and control characters. These codes usually conform to the American Standard Code for Information Interchange (ASCII).

text editor A program that is used to enter and modify text. In UNIX, `vi` is probably the most commonly-used text editor.

text entry mode A mode in a text editor that allows you to enter text.

text file A file that contains only text; also called a *document*.

text formatter A program that prepares text for printing, allowing you to produce indentation, margins, justification, headers, footers, pagination, and other forms of text enhancement. In UNIX, the basic text formatters are `nroff` (for character printers) and `troff` (for laser printers and phototypesetters). Other programs that handle specialized types of text include `eqn` and `neqn` (for mathematical expressions) and `tbl` (for tabular material). Macro packages derived from `nroff` and `troff` include `ms`, `me`, and `mm`. Macro packages provide ease of use for new users.

time-sharing A method of rotating processes that allows more than one user to have access to a computer system simultaneously. Each process is allocated a small segment of time in succession so that each user appears to have the computer to himself or herself. The amount of time assigned to each process is determined by a system of priorities.

troff A UNIX text formatting program, often mentioned together with its companion program `nroff`. While `nroff` (pronounced enroff) prepares text for printing on a character printer, `troff` (pronounced tee-roff) prepares text for printing on a laser printer or phototypesetter. These general-purpose formatters are accompanied by auxiliary programs that handle specialized types of text: `eqn` for mathematical expressions (with `troff`), `neqn` for mathematical expressions (with `nroff`), `tbl` for tabular material. To use one of the formatting programs, you must embed codes in a text file. These codes, most of which consist of a period followed by two letters, are interpreted by the formatters as commands. Commands for `nroff` and `troff` are called *requests*. A macro feature of `nroff` and `troff` lets you create your own custom requests. A complete set of these macros can form a macro package, which simplifies text formatting. Some of the most common macro packages include `ms` (the standard before System V), `me` (found in Berkeley systems), and `mm` (the standard for System V). The `mm` macro package is described in Chapter 7 of this book.

Trojan horse A scheme for breaking into a UNIX system, named after the trick used to end the Trojan war. In UNIX "warfare," a Trojan horse is a mock program, named after a real UNIX command, that helps an intruder carry out a later invasion. When a user or the system administrator unknowingly invokes the Trojan horse, it collects vital information, such as passwords or permissions, for use by the intruder.

229

tty An abbreviation for TeleType, which is used in UNIX to mean terminal. For example, `tty03` means terminal number 3.

typeface In printing, a set of characters that share a common design, though often in different styles. A set of characters with a particular typeface, style, and size is called a *font*.

typesetter See *phototypesetter*.

UNIX system A multiuser, multitasking operating system. Originally developed by Ken Thompson and Dennis Ritchie at Bell Laboratories in 1969, it has gradually gained wider acceptance since its simple beginnings. During the 1970s, the system was distributed to many universities throughout the United States. During the 1980s, the system has become a standard for the U. S. government and has been implemented by more and more computer manufacturers. One of the most attractive features of the UNIX system is its portability, which allows it to be run on computer systems of all sizes and brand names. Some of the drawbacks of the system include its cryptic command names and inconsistent rules of syntax. The name UNIX is taken from its predecessor, the Multics operating system. The UNIX system is described in this book.

Usenet A worldwide bulletin board that is available at sites that belong to the UUCP network. The bulletin board includes news groups for those interested in computer technology, recreation, science, social issues, and general discussion.

UUCP A set of programs and protocols that have become the basis of a worldwide network between UNIX systems; named after the UNIX-to-UNIX copy program. The version that has accompanied UNIX since System V, Release 3 goes by one of two names: HoneyDanBer or Basic Networking Utilities. The word HoneyDanBer is derived from the names of its originators, Peter Honeyman, David A. Nowitz, and Brian E. Redman. UUCP is described in Chapter 6 of this book.

variable A symbolic name to which you can assign a value, which may vary from one instance to another.

vi The most popular UNIX text editor, which was developed at the University of California at Berkeley by William Joy. Actually, `vi` is the visual interpreter of the `ex` line editor. Because it is a full-screen editor, `vi` can operate properly only after your terminal has been identified and described to the system. The `vi` editor is described in Chapter 5 of this book.

wildcard A character, used to search for text, that may represent any character (or any character in a set). A wildcard character is like a wild card in a card game, which may represent any other card in the deck.

window An area of a video screen that is dedicated to a particular program or file. Many of the newer implementations of UNIX employ windows as an easy, graphical way to provide multi-tasking.

word processor A program that combines text-processing and text-formatting. In the UNIX system, text-processing and text-formatting are separate functions.

workstation A desktop computer system, often rich in graphical features, that is more powerful than an ordinary personal computer. While personal computers are mainly intended for business applications, workstations tend to be favored by scientists and engineers.

working directory The directory in which you are working; also known as the *current directory*.

XENIX An operating system, derived from UNIX, that was specifically designed for personal computers in the early 1980s. With the growing power of personal computers in the late 1980s, the need for a separate XENIX system is diminishing and AT&T and Microsoft Corporation are in the process of merging XENIX with UNIX.

231

Appendix B
Quick Reference

This appendix summarizes the function, syntax, and some of the most common options for each command described in this book. The number (or numbers) on the right indicate the page (or pages) on which the command is described.

---

bc   *pages 91–92*

Start the high-precision calculator

```
$ bc [options] [files]
```

Option	Function
-l	Invoke the math library

Command	Function
+	Add
−	Subtract
*	Multiply
/	Divide

Command	Function
sqrt	Take square root
scale	Request decimal places
define	Define a function
quit	End a session

---

cal   *pages 69–70*

Display a calendar for a year or month

$ **cal** [*month*] [*year*]

234   in which

> *month* is a number from 1 to 12 (1 for January, 2 for February, 3 for March, and so on)
>
> *year* is a number from 1 to 9999 (representing a year A.D.)

---

calendar   *pages 129–130*

Send a reminder to yourself

$ **calendar** [-] [*year*]

Option	Function
–	Run calendar for all users who have calendar files

cat
pages 30, 71–72

Display the contents of a file; concatenate files

`$ cat [options] files`

Option	Function
-s	Suppress messages about nonexistent files
-u	Unbuffer output (Release 3)
-v	Display nonprinting characters (Release 3)
-t	With -v only, display tab as ^I (Release 3)
-e	With -v only, display $ at the end of each line (Release 3)

235

cd
pages 26–27

Change directories (move from one directory to another)

`$ cd [directory]`

If you omit a directory name, move to your home directory

chmod

pages 38–40

Set file permissions

```
$ chmod [augo][+-=][rwx] files
```

or

```
$ chmod number files
```

Option	Function
a	All (user, group, and others) (the default)
u	The user (or owner)
g	The user's working group
o	Other users (outside the user's group)
+	Add permission
–	Remove permission
=	Assign permissions absolutely
r	Permission to read
w	Permission to write
x	Permission to execute

236

cp

pages 29–30

Copy a file (or a group of files)

```
$ cp source_file target_file
```

or

```
$ cp files directory
```

cpio   *pages 182–188*

Back up and recover files

    $ cpio –o [aBcv]   Copy out

or

    $ cpio –i [Bcdfmrtuv]   Copy in
    [*text*]

or

    $ cpio –p [adlmruv]   Pass
    directory

Option	Function
a	Update access times of input files after copying
B	Copy in blocks of 5,120 bytes per record
c	Include ASCII header information
d	Create directories as required
f	Copy all files except those named in *text*
l	Link instead of copy whenever possible
m	Retain modification times already in effect
r	Rename files interactively (using prompts)
t	Table of contents: display names only
u	Copy the files unconditionally
v	Verbose: Display names of files being copied

237

cu   *pages 136–140*

Call another system

`$ cu [options] system`

Option	Function
-d	Display diagnostic messages
-e	Set even parity for sending
-l*line*	Select a line name (first available line if *line* is omitted)
-m	Select a direct line with modem control
-n	Number: prompt for a telephone number
-o	Set odd parity for sending
-s*rate*	Set the data rate to *rate* (300 bits per second by default)
-t	Call an ASCII terminal
system	You can use a telephone number or a uucp name

The following commands can be used in cu sessions:

Command	Function
~!	Escape from cu to the local shell
~!*command*	Run *command* on the local system
~$*command*	Run *command* on the local system and send output to the other system
~%cd	Change directories on local system (Release 2)
~%put *file*	Copy *file* to the other system
~%take *file*	Copy *file* from the other system
~.	Disconnect the two systems

dc

pages 90–91

Start the desk calculator

```
$ dc [file]
```

Command	Function
+	Add
–	Subtract
*	Multiply
/	Divide
p	Print (display)
q	Quit

239

egrep

See grep, pages 82–86

List lines in a file that meet criteria, including compound expressions

```
$ egrep [options] text [files]
```

Option	Function
-c	Count: display the number of matching lines
-e *expr*	Match an expression that begins with a hyphen
-f *file*	Read expressions from *file*
-i	Ignore case during search
-l	Display filenames only, not matching lines
-n	Display line numbers with matching lines
-v	Display nonmatching lines instead of matching lines

fgrep

See grep, pages 82–86

List lines in a file that meet criteria (literal strings only)

$ fgrep [*options*] *text* [*files*]

Option	Function
-c	Count: display the number of matching lines
-e *expr*	Match an expression that begins with a hyphen
-f *file*	Read expressions from *file*
-i	Ignore case during search
-l	Display filenames only, not matching lines
-n	Display line numbers with matching lines
-v	Display nonmatching lines instead of matching lines
-x	Match only entire lines

find

pages 78–82

List filenames that meet criteria

$ find *directories options*

Option	Function
-atime *d*	Match files accessed *d* days ago
-cpio *dev*	Write file to device *dev* using cpio format
-ctime *d*	Match files changed *d* days ago
-depth	List files before their directories
-exec *cmd*	Execute command *cmd* unconditionally

−group *name*	Match files that belong to group *name*
−links *n*	Match files with *n* links
−mtime *d*	Match files modified *d* days ago
−name *name*	Match files named *name*
−newer *name*	Match files newer than file *name*
−ok *cmd*	Execute command *cmd* with confirmation
−print	Display the names of all files matched
−size *b*	Match files that are *b* blocks long
−type *x*	Match files if *x*=p, directories if *x*=d
−user *name*	Match files owned by user *name*

grep

pages 82–86

241

List lines in a file that meet criteria, searching for strings and regular expressions

```
$ grep [options] text [files]
```

Option	Function
−c	Count: display the number of matching lines
−i	Ignore case during search
−l	Display filenames only, not matching lines
−n	Display line numbers with matching lines
−v	Display nonmatching lines rather than matching lines

ln

pages 33–36

Form a link to a file

```
$ ln source_file target_file
```

or

```
$ ln files directory
```

lp

pages 73–77

242

Queue a file (or a list of files) for printing

```
$ lp [options] files
```

Option	Function
-c	Make a copy of the file (or files) before printing it (or them)
-d*printer*	Direct printing to printer *printer*
-m	Mail message to user after printing
-n*copies*	Print the number of copies indicated (*copies*)
-t*message*	Print a message as a banner on the page that precedes the printed output
-w	Write a message to the user after printing

lpstat   *page 77*

Display the printing queue

```
$ lpstat [options]
```

Option	Function
-c[*items*]	Display classes and printers (*items*=names of classes)
-d	Display the name of the default printer
-o[*items*]	Display the status of printing requests (*items*=names of classes, names of printers, or identifiers of printing requests)
-p[*items*]	Display the status of printers (*items*=names of printers)
-r	Display the status of the request scheduler
-s	Display a summary of printing status (options -cdru combined)
-t	Display all status information
-u[*items*]	Display the status of print requests (*items*=login names of users)
-v[*items*]	Display printers with their pathnames (*items*=printers)

243

Note: In each instance, the items listed must be separated by commas.

ls   *pages 25–26, 36–38*

Display (or list) the contents of a directory

```
$ ls [options] [file]
```

in which

> *file* can be the name of a file or a directory

244

Option	Function
-a	Display all filenames (including those that begin with periods, such as .profile)
-C	Display filenames in multiple columns sorted from top to bottom
-F	Display a slash (/) at the end of each directory name and an asterisk (*) at the end of the name of each executable file
-l	Display a long list in seven columns
-n	Display a long list with numeric entries for user and group
-p	Display a slash (/) at the end of each directory name
-r	Display in reverse order
-t	Display filenames by time of last modification
-u	Display filenames by time of last access
-x	Display filenames in multiple columns sorted from left to right

mail (Release 2)   *pages 130–132*

Send electronic mail to another user; receive mail

```
$ mail [options] [users]
```

Option	Function
–e	Don't show mail
–f *file*	Read from *file* instead of the default mail file
–p	Display all incoming mail without prompts
–r	Display mail in reverse order
–t	Precede your message with the names of all recipients

245

Code	Action
* (or ?)	List all the mail commands
p	Redisplay the current message (print)
d	Delete the current message
m *user*	Forward the current message to *user*
s	Save the current message (with header) in file mbox
s *file*	Save the current message (with header) in *file*
w	Save the current message (without header) in file mbox
w *file*	Save the current message (without header) in *file*
Enter	Display the next message
! *command*	Execute *command* without leaving mail
q	Quit mail (leave only unexamined messages)
x	Exit mail (leave all messages)

mail (Release 3)   *pages 130–132*

Send electronic mail to another user; receive mail

```
$ mail [options] [users]
```

Option	Send Function
-o	Don't use address optimization
-s	Don't begin with a newline at the top
-t	Add a To: line to your message
-w	For remote mail, don't wait for completion of remote transfer program

Option	Receive Function
-e	Don't show the mail
-F *user*	Forward mail to *users*
-h	Show a numbered list of messages
-f *file*	Read from *file* instead of the default mail file
-p	Display all incoming mail without prompts
-r	Display mail in reverse order

Code	Action
?	List all the mail commands
n	Display message *n*
p	Redisplay the current message (print)
d	Delete the current message
dq	Delete the current message and quit
d *n*	Delete message *n*
m *user*	Forward the current message to *user*
s	Save the current message (with header) in file mbox
s *file*	Save the current message (with header) in *file*

w	Save the current message (without header) in file `mbox`
w *file*	Save the current message (without header) in *file*
−	Display the previous message
+	Display the next message
Enter	Display the next message
h	Display some headers, including the current header
h a	Display all headers
h d	Display headers for messages to be deleted
h *n*	Display header for message *n*
! *command*	Execute *command* without leaving `mail`
q	Quit `mail` (leave only unexamined messages)
x	Exit `mail` (leave all messages)

247

mailx   *pages 132–135*

Send electronic mail to another user; receive mail

`$ mailx [`*options*`] [`*users*`]`

Option	Function
−e	Check for mail without reading it
−H	Display headers without messages
−N	Display messages without headers
−s *hdr*	Set subject header to *hdr*
−U	Convert from `uucp` to `mailx`

Command	Action
~?	List all escape commands
~s *subject*	Enter a subject title called *subject*

Command	Action
~t *user(s)*	Add users to the To list
~c *user(s)*	Add users to the Copy list
~h	Display To, Subject, and Copy prompts
~r *file*	Read text into your message from another file
~w *file*	Write your message to another file
~v	Use vi to edit your message
~p	Display (print) the current message
~f *message(s)*	Read in other messages
~m *message(s)*	Read in other messages (indented to the first tab stop)
~! *command*	Run a UNIX command and return to mailx
~¦ *command*	Pipe the message through *command* (UNIX command)
~q	Quit mailx (save message in file dead.letter)
~x	Exit mailx (discard message)

248

Command	Action
?	List all commands with explanations
list	List all commands without explanations
header	Display active headers
z	Display the next page of headers
z –	Display the last page of headers
from [*list*]	Display header(s)
top [*list*]	Display only the first five lines of message(s)
next	Display the next message
type [*list*]	Display message(s)
preserve [*list*]	Preserve message(s) in mbox

`save [list] file`	Save message(s) (append) to *file*
`delete [list]`	Delete message(s)
`undelete [list]`	Undelete deleted message(s)
`edit [list]`	Edit message(s)
`Reply [list]`	Reply to sender(s) only
`reply [list]`	Reply to sender(s) and to other recipients
`cd [directory]`	Change to *directory* (home if name omitted)
`! command`	Execute UNIX command and return to `mailx`
`quit`	Quit (save only unread messages in `mbox`)
`xit`	Exit (save all messages in `mbox`)

249

mesg   *page 129*

Determine whether or not other users can send messages directly to your screen

| `$ mesg y` | Allow incoming messages |
| `$ mesg n` | Forbid incoming messages |

mkdir   *pages 27–28*

Create a new subdirectory under the current directory

`$ mkdir directory`

mm

pages 155–156

Format text for printing

```
$ mm [options] file(s)
```

Request	Function
.P 0	Block paragraph
.P 1	Paragraph with indented first line
.DS *option*	Static display
.DF *option*	Floating display
I	Indented
I F *n*	Double-indented
C	Centered
CB	Blocked
.BL	Bullet list
.DL	Dash list
.ML *mark*	Mark list
.RL	Reference list
.VL	Variable-item list
.AL	Auto-number list
.SA 1	Justify text
.SA 0	Unjustify text
.SP *n*	Skip *n* lines
.I	Make text italic
.B	Make text bold
.R	Make text roman
.S *p v*	Change point size and line spacing

mv   *pages 30–32*

Rename a file (or files); move a file (or files)

```
$ mv source_file target_file
```

or

```
$ mv files directory
```

nroff   *page 154*

Format text for printing (fixed width)

251

```
$ nroff [options] [files]
```

Option	Function
-cx	Process with macro package m x
-e	Space words equally in justified text
-opages	Print only *pages* as listed here
-Tprinter	Specify a particular printer
p1-p2	Print from page *p1* to page *p2*
-p	Print from beginning of file to page *p*
p-	Print from page *p* to the end of the file

Request	Function
.pl n	Page length *n* lines
.po n	Page offset *n* characters
.pn n	Page number *n*
.bp	Page break
.ll n	Line length *n* characters
.in n	Indent *n* characters
.ti n	Temporarily indent *n* characters

Request	Function
`.ne` *n*	Need vertical space (*n* lines)
`.fi`	Turn on filling
`.nf`	Turn off filling
`.ad`	Adjust text
`.na`	Do not adjust text
`.hy` *n*	Hyphenate after *n* characters
`.nh`	No hyphenation
`.br`	Break to a new page
`.ls` *n*	Line spacing *n*
`.ce`	Center a line
`.ce` *n*	Center the next *n* lines
`.ul`	Underline text
`.cu`	Continuously underline text
`%`	Place page number
`\u`	Superscript
`\d`	Subscript
`.1C`	Single column
`.2C`	Double column
`.TS`	Start of table
`.TE`	End of table
`.EQ`	Start of equation
`.EN`	End of equation

252

passwd page 15

Change your password

```
$ passwd
Changing password for user
Old password:
New password:
Retype new password:
$ _
```

pg *pages 72–73*

Display text one screenful at a time

```
$ pg [options] [files]
```

Option	Function
-c	Home cursor and clear screen each page
-e	Do not pause at the end of a file
-f	Do not split lines wider than screen
-n	Allow one-letter commands without pressing Enter
-s	Highlight prompts and messages
+*line*	Start at line number *line*
+/*string*/	Start at the first line that contains *string*
p	Go to the previous file
n	Go to the next file
–	Move to the previous screen
+	Move to the next screen
Enter	Move to the next screen
-*n*l	Move back *n* lines
+*n*l	Move forward *n* lines
?*text*?	Move to the previous line that contains *text*
/*text*/	Move to the next line that contains *text*

253

ps *page 55*

Check the status of processes

```
$ ps [options]
```

Option	Function
-a	Display all processes except process group leaders and processes not started from terminals
-d	Display all processes except process group leaders
-e	Display all processes, not just your own
-f	Produce a "full" list
-l	Produce a "long" list

pwd

page 27

254

Display the name of your current directory

```
$ pwd
/usr/james/admin/letters
$ _
```

readnews

page 147

Read the Usenet bulletin board

```
$ readnews [options] [newgroups]
```

Option	Action
?	Help
N	Go to the next newsgroup
U	Unsubscribe from the current newsgroup
b	Back up one article in the current newsgroup
-	Return to the previous article
+	Skip the current article

e	Erase the memory of having read the current article
s *file*	Save the current article in *file*
r	Reply to the author of an article
f	Post a follow-up to an article
Del	Throw away the rest of an article
x	Exit

Example:

```
$ readnews -n rec.games.chess rec.pets
```

rm   *pages 32–33* **255**

Delete a file (or a group of files)

```
$ rm [options] files
```

Option	Function
-f	Remove files from directories forcibly
-i	Remove files interactively (using prompts)
-r	Used with a directory name, remove all subdirectories and files, then remove the directory itself

rmdir   *page 28*

Delete (or remove) an existing directories

```
$ rmdir directories
```

Option	Function
-p	Remove directories along with any parent directories that may become empty (Release 3), and display the names of all directories removed
-r	Delete files from directories recursively
-s	Used with -p, don't display directory names

---

sh

pages 62–64

Shell (the command processor)

```
$ sh [script]
```

Shell Variables

Bourne and C shells	
HOME	Login directory
MAIL	Mail file
PATH	Command search path
TERM	Terminal type

Bourne shell only	
PS1	Primary prompt
PS2	Secondary prompt
IFS	Internal file separator
TZ	Time zone
LOGNAME	Login name

Command	Function
<	Redirect command input
>	Redirect command output
>>	Redirect and append to an output file
&	Run a background process
echo *text*	Display *text* on the video monitor
read *var*	Receive text from the keyboard and assign it to variable *var*
ps	Display the status of background processes
nice *n*	Change the priority of a process
kill *pppp*	Terminate background process *pppp*
shl	Use the shell layer manager
p1 ¦ *p2*	Pipe: Use output of *p1* as the input of *p2*
p ¦ tee *file*	Tee: Display the output of *p* while it is being redirected to *file*

257

Matching Patterns

?	Match any one character
*	Match any string of characters
[*characters*]	Match any of the characters enclosed

Positional Parameters

$0	Command
$1	First argument
$2	Second argument
$3	Third argument
...	
$*n*	The *n*th argument

sort

pages 86–90

Sort lines in a file; merge sorted files

```
$ sort [options] [files]
```

Option	Function
-b	Ignore spaces and tabs in front of text
-c	Make sure file has already been sorted
-d	Sort in dictionary order
-f	"Fold" uppercase into lowercase
-m	Merge files that have already been sorted
-M	Sort items as months (Jan, Feb, Mar, ...)
-n	Sort in numeric order
-o *file*	Place output in *file*
-r	Sort in reverse order
-u	Unique: if identical lines occur, output only one
+*n*	Begin sorting after *n* fields
-*m*	Stop sorting after *m* fields

258

su

page 175

Change to another login name

```
$ su name      Change to user name
Password:
$ _

$ su           Change to root
Password:
# _
```

tee   *pages 52–53*

Redirect output to a file while sending it to the standard output

```
$ tee [options] [files]
```

Option	Function
-a	Append to a file (similar to >>)
-i	Ignore the signal from the Del key, which usually interrupts processing

Appendix C
The C Shell

In Chapter 3, "Processing Commands," you learned how to use the command processors, known as the Bourne shell and the C shell. This appendix presents several features of the C shell that are not found in the Bourne shell:

- ▶ Using the C shell initialization files
- ▶ Setting the shell prompt
- ▶ Retrieving previous command lines
- ▶ Creating customized commands

C Shell Initialization Files

While the Bourne shell has a single initialization file called `.pro-file`, the C shell has two initialization files named `.login` and `.cshrc`. The `.login` file is similar to `.profile`, but `.cshrc` is unique to the C shell. Although the system reads `.cshrc` before `.login` when you first log in, let's first discuss `.login`.

The Login File   *.login*

The .login file, which is read and executed only when you log in, contains the basic information that allows your terminal to function properly. The statements placed here are similar to those placed in .profile for the Bourne shell, but the commands and syntax are slightly different for the C shell. Here is an example of a simple .login file, which contains three lines:

```
stty kill "^A" erase "^H"
setenv TERM vt100
set path=(/bin /usr/bin $HOME/bin .)
```

The first line contains a command that sets the terminal, stty, which is described in Chapter 8. This line assigns Ctrl-A as the kill key and Ctrl-H as the erase key. (As you may recall, the kill key is the key combination that erases an entire command line, and the erase key is the one that erases the previous character.)

The second line contains a command that identifies your terminal to the system by assigning a value to the TERM variable. The value assigned on this line (vt100) must be listed in the appropriate place in the terminal information file that is used on your system (either /etc/termcap or /usr/lib/terminfo/v/vt100).

The third line sets up your command search path, using a construction that differs from the one used by the Bourne shell. Assuming that your home directory is /usr/paul, the system will search for command names in the following directories:

```
/bin
/usr/bin
/usr/paul/bin
```

The C Shell Run Command File   *.cshrc*

The .cshrc file is unique to the C shell; it is read and executed each time the system creates a new C shell, which occurs both when you first log in and also when you start a C shell procedure. The .cshrc file is generally used to do three things:

Set your shell prompt

Set the number of command lines to be saved for future reference, referred to as a *history*

Create custom commands, known as *aliases*

The following example of a simple .cshrc file contains five lines:

```
set prompt = "\!> "
set history = 10
alias     t        cd /usr/lib/terminfo/v
alias     u        cd /usr/lib/uucppublic/paul
alias     show     cd '\!*; ls -l | pg'
```

The first line sets your prompt. Although you can always use the default prompt for the C shell (%), it can be much more convenient to use sequential numbers that count your command lines for you. Then you can refer to previous command lines by number. In this example, the exclamation mark preceded by a backslash specifies the dynamic numbering of command lines. When you log in with this setting in your .cshrc file, your first shell prompt will look like this:

263

```
1> _
```

In the terminology of the C shell, each command line is called an *event*, and the set of command lines stored for future reference is called the *history* list. The second line in the example .cshrc file specifies the length of the history list (10). This means that the system will save the previous ten command lines, or events, for reference. Because you have requested line-numbering, it will be easy for you to refer to events by number.

Each system limits the maximum number of events allowed in a history list. For most systems, the limit is around 25 events. You can also change the setting for the variable history on a command line, as shown here:

```
1> set history = 5
2> _
```

From this point on, the system will retain only five events at a time. Later, if you want to view the events stored, you can execute the history command:

```
21> history
    16   cd ../admin
    17   pwd
    18   ls -l
    19   mv letter ltr.427
    20   vi ltr.427
22> _
```

As you will learn shortly, you can retrieve any one of these events, run it again, or modify it and run it.

To permit us to retrieve a larger number of events, let's make the history list ten events long by executing another set history command. Although this setting was in .cshrc, the following command makes certain it is in effect:

```
22> set history = 10
23> _
```

264

The last three lines of the sample .cshrc file contain aliases. An alias is simply an abbreviation that you can assign to an existing command (usually a long, complex command). For example, the alias shown on the third line lets you enter

```
2> t
```

rather than

```
2> cd /usr/lib/terminfo/v
```

whenever you want to change to the terminfo directory indicated. The alias saves time by allowing you to use a shorter name.

Now that we've briefly discussed the .cshrc file, let's look at some of the features in more detail.

Retrieving Command Lines

The ability to retrieve any event in the history list is a great convenience that can save you time. Some command lines are very long and easy to mistype. The most common ways you can retrieve a command line are as follows:

Invoke the previous event

Invoke an event by actual line number

To invoke either of these, you must first type an exclamation mark (!). Because of this special meaning, you have to use an escape (\) any time you use an exclamation mark for any other purpose in the C shell. You saw an example of this in the notation used to set up line-numbering in the .cshrc file.

Repeating the Previous Event   !!

The simplest command you can use is !!, which repeats the most recent event (re-executes the most recent command line). Suppose you are right where you left off in the previous section (checking the history list). If you enter !! now, the history command will be executed again:

265

```
22> !!
history
     16   cd ../admin
     17   pwd
     18   ls -l
     19   mv letter ltr.427
     20   vi ltr.427
23> _
```

You can display the history list a second time by entering !! rather than history. The C shell displays the command line and then the results of the command line.

Invoking an Event by Number   !n

To illustrate this feature, let's repeat command line 17. In this instance, you won't save any keystrokes. However, in most instances, you probably will. This is how it will look on your screen:

```
25> !17
pwd
/usr/paul/admin
26> _
```

Merely type an exclamation mark, followed by the number of the event desired (in this example, 17).

 To use a filename that you have just generated, type !$.

Selecting Arguments on a Command Line

In Chapter 3, "Command Processing," you learned that the Bourne shell splits each command line into individual units and assigns them numbers. The C shell also does this. For example, consider the following command line:

```
19> mv letter ltr.427
```

This command line contains the following three units, or *words*:

mv	Word 0 ($0): the command
letter	Word 1 ($1): the first argument
ltr.427	Word 2 ($2): the second argument

The C shell allows you to select from these words when you invoke an event in your history list. Simply append a colon and a number to your repeat command. For example, to use the filename ltr.427 as an argument in another command line, you could use the following notation:

```
26> cat !19:2
cat ltr.427              First, the C shell interprets the
                         notation.

May 18, 1991
Dear Fred,               Then it displays the output.
...
Sincerely,
Paul
27> _
```

266

The command line on line 26 means, "Use the second argument on line 19 as the argument for the `cat` command."

In the sections that follow, you will learn how to select an individual argument (as in the previous command) or a series of arguments. To make the discussion easy to follow, we'll use the following command line throughout:

```
27> echo arg-1 arg-2 arg-3 arg-4 arg-5
arg-1 arg-2 arg-3 arg-4 arg-5
28> _
```

Selecting the First Argument   ^

You can use either the number one (1) or a caret symbol (^) to select the first argument. The following example uses the number one:

267

```
28> echo !27:1
echo arg-1
arg-1
29> _
```

The example that follows is equivalent to the previous example:

```
28> echo !27:^
echo arg-1
arg-1
29> _
```

Selecting the Last Argument $

The symbol for selecting the last argument ($) is much more useful that the one for selecting the first argument because you may not know exactly how many arguments there are. In the following example, the dollar sign ($) is equivalent to 5:

```
29> echo !27:$
echo arg-5
arg-5
30> _
```

Selecting a Set of Arguments   *n1-n2*

You can use a hyphen (–) between a pair of numbers to select a
range of arguments. In the following example we select arguments
2, 3, and 4:

```
30> echo !27:2-4
echo arg-2 arg-3 arg-4
arg-2 arg-3 arg-4
31> _
```

Selecting All Arguments   *

If you want to select every argument on the command line, you
can use the wildcard character (*), as shown in the following
example:

```
31> echo !27:*
echo arg-1 arg-2 arg-3 arg-4 arg-5
arg-1 arg-2 arg-3 arg-4 arg-5
32> _
```

Because you are using the same command on line 31 that you
used on line 27, command line 31 could be entered more simply
as follows:

```
31> !27
echo arg-1 arg-2 arg-3 arg-4 arg-5
arg-1 arg-2 arg-3 arg-4 arg-5
32> _
```

However, if you were using a different command on line 31,
the wildcard notation would be very handy.

Simplified Notation

The C shell allows you to omit the colon (:) any time you are
using symbols instead of numbers to select arguments. In other
words, command lines 28, 29, and 31 could be entered more simply as follows:

```
28> echo !27^
echo arg-1
arg-1
29> echo !27$
echo arg-5
arg-5
30> ...

31> echo !27*
echo arg-1 arg-2 arg-3 arg-4 arg-5
arg-1 arg-2 arg-3 arg-4 arg-5
32> _
```

With numbers, however, you always must include the colon
(:) when selecting arguments.

Changing a Command Line

269

To avoid unnecessary typing, you can modify an event when you
invoke it. Merely type the appropriate modifier after the colon (:)
rather than numbers or symbols to select arguments.

Making Substitutions   *s*

The C shell's substitute modifier s is similar to vi's substitute
command s (if necessary, refer to Chapter 5, "Editing with vi").
Let's repeat event number 27 and append the modifier s/a/A:

```
32> !27:s/a/A
echo Arg-1 arg-2 arg-3 arg-4 arg-5
Arg-1 arg-2 arg-3 arg-4 arg-5
33> _
```

As the preceding example shows, the s modifier by itself
replaces only the first occurrence on the line. It changed arg-1 to
Arg-1, but the other four arguments were unchanged.

If you want to replace a with A everywhere on the line, you
have to include the global modifier g, as shown in the following
example:

```
33> !27:gs/a/A
echo Arg-1 Arg-2 Arg-3 Arg-4 Arg-5
Arg-1 Arg-2 Arg-3 Arg-4 Arg-5
34> _
```

To make a replacement only in one argument, you can include the argument number and also the s modifier, each with its own colon. In the following example, we change arg to ARG only in argument number 3:

```
34> !27:3:s/arg/ARG
echo ARG-3
ARG-3
35> _
```

Previewing an Event   *p*

270

If you want to look at an event without executing it, merely append the preview modifier p. Here is an example:

```
35> !27:p
echo arg-1 arg-2 arg-3 arg-4 arg-5
36> _
```

Using Abbreviations   **alias**

The last three lines of the sample .cshrc file described earlier in this chapter contained *alias* commands. For this example, these three lines constitute an alias list. On the fourth line, we assigned to u the command line cd /usr/lib/uucppublic/paul. Therefore you can enter

```
36> u
37> _
```

rather than

```
36> cd /usr/lib/uucppublic/paul
37> _
```

Displaying the Alias List

You can display your alias list at any time by executing the `alias` command alone, as follows:

```
37> alias
alias       t          cd /usr/terminfo/v
alias       u          cd /usr/lib/uucppublic/paul
alias       show       cd '\!*; ls -l | pg'
38> _
```

Using a Temporary Alias

The aliases stored in .cshrc go into effect each time you log in or create a new C shell. If you want to set up an alias for one session, you can assign it and then remove it, as shown in this example:

271

```
38> alias s  cd /usr/sandy/sales
39> s
...
43> s
...
47> s
...
55> unalias s
...
56> _
```

In the preceding example, you assign an alias called s on line 38, use the alias three times (lines 39, 43, and 47), and then remove the alias on line 55.

Using Dynamic Selection   \!*

The fifth line of the initialization file .cshrc includes a provision for dynamic selection. All this means is that you can enter the target directory name at the time you enter your command line. The alias line reads as follows:

```
alias       show       cd '\!*; ls -l ¦ pg'
```

In this example, we assign to the name show a command line that lets us change to any directory and display a long listing of files. The notation \!* simply means, "Enter any name here." This would be another way of showing the desired command line:

```
cd directory; ls -l ¦ pg
```

The following example uses the alias show:

```
56> show /usr/alfred/times
cd /usr/alfred/times; ls -l ¦ pg
total 52
drwx--x---   2  alfred             758  Jul 18  15:42  anderson
-rwxr-x---   1  alfred             292  Feb 20  09:14  archer.tm
drwx--x---   1  alfred             326  Nov 31  08:57  bell_sale
-rw-r-----   3  alfred             615  Aug  3  13:09  carter.ne
-rw-r-----   1  alfred             961  May 11  10:38  dale_two
...
: _
```

Answers to Quizzes

Answers for Chapter 1

1. D	2. A	3. True	4. B	5. C
6. C	7. D	8. B	9. A	10. D

Answers for Chapter 2

1. F	2. I	3. C	4. B	5. G	6. A
7. D	8. J	9. H	10. E	11. L	12. K

13.   `cp memo.? ../MEMOS`
14.   `cd ..`
15.   `mv *.G ../sales`
16.   `ls -l`
17.   `ln /usr/paul/LETTERS/expedite expedite`
18.   `mkdir news`
19.   `chmod u+x,g+w,o-rwx meeting`
20.   `rm interest.[KNR]`

Answers for Chapter 3

1. A	2. C	3. B	4. D	5. A
6. B	7. C	8. B	9. D	10. C
11. T	12. D	13. C	14. B	15. A

Answers for Chapter 4

1. E	2. B	3. A	4. G	5. C
6. F	7. D			

8. `cal 10 1562`

9.
```
cat > test.doc
This is a very,
very small file.
Ctrl-D
$ _
```

10. `lp -m memo.101 memo.102`

11. `find /usr -user penny -atime 30`

12. `grep "006[0-9][1-9]" parts.*`

13. `sort +3 parts.* > parts.price`

14. `sort +2 -3 parts.* > parts.partno`

15.
```
bc
scale = 5
sqrt(500)
22.36068
quit
```

Answers for Chapter 5

1. H	2. E	3. A	4. I	5. L	6. D
7. B	8. J	9. C	10. G	11. K	12. F
13. D	14. F	15. E	16. A	17. C	18. B

19. E	20. H	21. B	22. D	23. F	24. A
25. J	26. C	27. I	28. G	29. 5dd	30. d$
31. d^	32. d5}	33. 5x	34. /select	35. p	36. :1,$s/ select/ choose/g

Answers for Chapter 6

1. D	2. G	3. B	4. E	5. J	6. A
7. I	8. F	9. C	10. H		

```
11.    write sean < hello
12.    mesg n
13.    calendar
14.    mail linda mike paula < urgent
15.    mailx
16.    reply
17.    cu gemini
18.    cu gemini | tee gemini.session
19.    mail minverva!ken
20.    cat sales.3Q | uux - minerva!lp
```

275

Answers for Chapter 7

1. G	2. F	3. B	4. E	5. D	6. A
7. C	8. E	9. L	10. A	11. U	12. J
13. W	14. P	15. R	16. B	17. S	18. V
19. C	20. N	21. Q	22. D	23. K	24. F
25. T	26. O	27. M	28. H	29. I	30. G
31. .DS C	32. .B	33. .R	34. .DE	35. .P □	36. .BL
37. .LI	38. .LI	39. .LI	40. .LE	41. .P □	42. .DS I
43. .B	44. .R	45. .DE	46. .P □	47. .I	

Answers for Chapter 8

1.	`root`	6.	`/dev`
2.	`su`	7.	`/usr/lib/crontab`
3.	`/etc`	8.	`chmod`
4.	`/etc/passwd`	9.	`ls	cpio -oB > /dev/rmt/3`
5.	`who`	10.	`ls	cpio -o > /dev/rdsk/1c0d1s0`

11. `cpio -iB < /dev/rmt/3`
12. `cpio -i < /dev/rdsk/c0d1s0`
13. `cpio -pv`
14. `stty 1200`
15. `stty erase = ^h kill = ^e`
16. `stty -raw`
17. `/etc/termcap`
18. `/usr/lib/terminfo`
19. `TERM`
20. `TERM = wyse50; export TERM`
21. `setenv TERM wyse50`
22. `.profile` (Bourne shell); `.login` (C shell)
23. `30 9 * * 5 cat /usr/paul/news > /dev/tty07`
24. `chmod 755 repeat`

276

Index

\# key (erase character), 16

\# prompt, 13

$ metacharacter, 85-86

$ prompt, 13

$TERM, 227

% prompt, 13

* wildcard character, 34-36, 85-86

? wildcard character, 34-36

@ (kill) key, 17

A

absolute pathname, 205

access, 205

account, 205

addresses, 205

   uucp networks, 142-144

alias C shell command, 205, 270-272

append, 206

append mode, 206

appending text, 109-110

arguments, 16, 46, 206

   C shell, 266-270

ASCII, 206

assign, 206

AT&T UNIX, 9-10

auto number lists, 163-165

B

background processes, 53-55, 206

   checking, 55

   requesting, 54-55

   terminating, 55-56

backing up files, 182-188

backslash, 206

backspace (erase character) key, 16

backup, 207

base 2 (binary) numbering, 198-199

base 8 (octal) numbering, 198-199

basename, 207

batch processing, 207

baud rate, 207

bc (high precision calculator) command, 91-92, 233-234

Berkeley UNIX BSD, 9-10, 207

bin directory, 22-23, 207

binary (base 2) numbering, 198-199

bit, 207

block, 207

bold text, 167-168, 207

boot, 207

Bourne shell, 43-44, 207

braces, 208

brackets, 208

BSD, 208

buffer, 208

bug, 208

bullet lists, 160
bulletin boards *see* Usenet
bus, 208
byte, 208

C

-c printing option, 75
C language, 209
C shell, 44, 211
   arguments, 266-270
   command syntax, 266-270
   commands
      alias, 270-272
      history, 263-265
   history list, 263-265
   intitialization files, 261-265
C shell files
   .cshrc (Run Command), 262-264
   .login, 262
CAE (Common Applications
   Environment), 11
cal (calendar) command, 69-70, 234
calculators
   desk, 90-91
   high-precision, 91-92
calendar command, 129-130, 234
calendars, 69-70
capturing electronic mail sessions,
   139
carriage return, 208
case, 208
cat (concatenate) command, 30,
   71-72, 235
cd (change directory) command, 26,
   235
changing passwords, 15
changing permissions, 38-40
character, 208
child process, 209
chip, 209
chmod (change mode) command,
   38-40, 197, 236
command line, 15-16, 45-46, 209

positional parameters, 58-59
command name, 209
command processor, 209
command syntax, C shell, 266-270
commands
   arguments, 16
   arguments, 46
   bc (high precision calculator),
      91-92, 233-234
   cal (calendar), 69-70, 234
   calendar, 129-130, 234
   cat (concatenate), 30, 71-72, 235
   cd (change directory), 26, 235
   chmod (change mode), 38-40,
      197, 236
   command line, 15-16, 45-46,
      58-59
   compared to processes, 47
   cp (copy), 29-30, 236
   cpio (copy I/O), 182-188, 211, 237
      -i, 186
      -o, 183-186
      -p, 187-188
   cron (system timer), 195-196, 211
   cu (call up), 136-140, 238
   date, 14
   dc (desk calculator), 90-91, 239
   dd, 188
   dump, 188
   egrep, 239
   entering, 14, 45-46
   fgrep, 240
   find, 78-82, 240-241
      action statements, 81-82
      switches, 79-82
   grep, 82-85, 241
   kill, 55-56
   ln (link), 33-34, 242
   lp (lineprinter), 73-77, 242
   lpstat (lineprinter status), 77, 243
   ls (list), 25-26, 244
   ls -l (list -long), 25-26, 36-37
   mail, 48-49, 130-132, 245-247
      options, 131-132

278

mailx, 132-135, 247-249
  ? commands, 135
  escape commands, 133-134
  options, 133-135
mesg (message), 129, 249
mkdir (make directory), 27-28, 249
more, 73
mv (move), 30-32, 251
nroff (new runoff), 251-252
passwd (password), 15, 252
pg (page), 72, 253
ps (process status), 55, 253-254
pwd (print working directory), 27, 223, 254
readnews, 254-255
restor, 188
rm (remove), 32-33, 255
rmdir (remove directory), 28, 255-256
setenv (set environment), 64
sh (shell), 256-257
sort, 86-90, 258
stty, 189-194
su (substitute user), 175, 226, 258
sync, 200, 227
tar (tape archive), 188, 227
tee, 52-53, 139-140, 259
uucp (UNIX-to-UNIX copy), 136-137, 140-144
uuname, 137-138
uux, 144-145
vi (visual interpreter), 95-124, 230
  / (search), 119-120
  a (append), 109-110
  d) (delete sentence), 114-115
  dd (delete line), 113-114
  dw (delete word), 112-113
  d} (delete paragraph), 115-116
  i (insert), 108-109
  o (open new line), 110-111
  p (put), 117-118
  s (substitute), 120-121
  subcommand tables, 122-124
  x (delete character), 112
volcopy, 188
wall (write-all), 176-177
who, 14, 181-182
write, 128-129
Common Applications Environment (CAE) *see* CAE
communicating with users, 176-177
communications
  system-to-system, 136-138
  terminal-to-terminal, 128-129
  UNIX-to-UNIX, 140-144
compiler, 210
computer, 210
concatenate, 210
configurations
  PC-based systems, 6-8
  stand-alone workstations, 6-8
  terminals and minicomputer, 6
  workstations in local area network, 6-7
configure, 210
connecting processes, 51-53
console, 210
constant, 210
control character, 210
controller, 210
conversions
  numeric, 198-199
cooked mode, 210
copying files, 29-30
  electronic mail, 138
core, 210
core dump, 211
cp (copy) command, 29-30, 236
cpio (copy I/O) command, 182-188, 237, 211
  -i, 186
  -o, 183-186
  -p, 187-188
crash, 211
creating directories, 27-28
cron (system timer) command, 195-196, 211

279

crontab, 211
CRT, 211
Crtl-D (log out) key, 17
Crtl-H (erase character) key, 16
cu (call up) command, 136-140, 238
cursor movement, 211
   text editor (vi command), 98-104

D

/dev/null device, 50
daemon processes, 195, 211
dash lists, 161
data, 211
data rate, 211
date command, 14
dc (desk calculator) command,
   90-91, 239
dd command, 188
debug, 211
decimal, 212
default, 212
Del key, 17
delete, 212
deleting
   directories, 28
   files, 32-33
   text, 112-116
desk calculator, 90-91
dev directory, 22-23
device, 212
device file, 212
devices, /dev/null, 50
directories, 25-27, 212
   /usr/spool/uucppublic, 143-144
   bin, 22-23
   changing, 26
   creating, 27-28
   deleting, 28
   dev, 22-23
   etc, 22-23, 175-176
   listing, 25-26
   ls (list) command, 25-26
   ls -l (list -long) command, 25-26

280

   mkdir (make directory) command,
     27-28
   pwd (print working directory)
     command, 27
   root, 22-23
   tmp, 22-23
   usr, 22-23
directory files, 24
disk, 212
displaying print queue, 77
displaying files, 72-73
document, 212
DOS, 3-5, 212
drive, 212
driver, 213
dump command, 188

E

/etc/group file, 178-180
/etc/passwd file, 177-180
echo, 213
ed, 213
edit, 213
editing text (vi command), 95-121
   appending text, 109-110
   command mode, 97
   cursor movement, 98-104
   deleting text, 112-116
   finding and replacing text,
     119-121
   inserting text, 108-109
   moving text, 116-118
   opening new lines, 110-111
   paging, 105
   repeating keystrokes, 100-101
   retrieving files, 99
   saving, 97
   scrolling, 105-106
   undoing keystrokes, 100-101
   zeroing screen, 106-107
editor, 213
egrep command, 239

electronic mail
   capturing sessions, 139
   copying files, 138
   mail command, 130-132
   mailx command, 132-135
   sending files, 138-139
   uucp networks, 141-144
entering commands, 14, 45-46
entering text, 72
environment, 62-64, 213
eqn, 213
erase character, 213
Esc key, 213
establishing user accounts, 177-180
etc directory, 22-23
ex, 213
examining files, 30
executable files, 56-62
execute, 213
expressions, 213
   regular, 85-86
extension, 214

F

fgrep command, 240
field, 214
field separator, 87-88, 214
fields, sorting, 87-88
file, 214
file system, 22-23, 214
   directories, 22-28
      bin, 22-23
      dev, 22-23
      etc, 22-23
      root, 22-23
      tmp, 22-23
      usr, 22-23
   files, 22-23
file type, 214
filename, 214
files
   .profile, 61-64
   /dev/null, 50

/etc/group, 178-180
/etc/passwd, 177-180
backing up, 182-188
C shell initialization, 261-265
copying, 29-30
   electronic mail, 138
deleting, 32-33
directory, 24
displaying, 72-73
examining, 30
executable, 56-62
finding, 78-82
   search criteria, 79-81
joining, 71-72
linking, 33-34
motd (message of the day), 177
moving, 30-32
names, 23-24
ordinary, 24
permissions, 36-40, 197-199
renaming, 30
search criteria, 79-81
searching for text, 82-86
security, 36-40
sending electronic mail, 138-139
sharing, 33-34
sorting fields, 87-88
sorting text, 86-90
special, 24
termcap, 227
termcap (terminal capability),
   191-194, 227
terminfo (terminal information),
   191-194, 228
types, 24
filter, 214
find command, 78-82, 240-241
   action statements, 81-82
   switches, 79-82
foreground, 214
foreground processes, 53
format, 214
formatting text, 153-167
   display, 157-159

281

lists, 160-165
    paragraphs, 156-157
full duplex, 214

G

global, 215
grep command, 82-85, 215, 224
group, 215

H

half-duplex, 215
hardware, 215
hardwired terminal, 215
hexadecimal, 215
high precision calculator, 91-92
high-level language, 215
highlighting text, 167-168
history, 215, 263-265
history list, C shell, 263-265
home (home directory) shell
    variable, 63
home directory, 215
host, 215

I

I/O, 216
indent, 215
input, 215
    redirecting, 47-51
insert mode, 215
inserting text, 108-109
install, 216
interactive processing, 216
interactive shell scripts, 59-61
italic text, 167-168, 216

J–K

joining files, 71-72
justify, 216
justifying text, 166
kernel, 54, 216

keys
    # (erase character), 16
    @ (kill), 17
    backspace (erase character), 16
    Crtl-D (log out), 17
    Crtl-H (erase character), 16
    Del, 17
    Esc, 213
    Shift-3 (erase character), 16
kill character, 216
kill command, 55-56
Korn shell, 44, 216

L

LAN *see* local area network
laser printer, 216
link, 216
linking files, 33-34
lists
    auto number, 163-165
    bullet, 160
    dash, 161
    mark, 161-162
    reference, 162
    variable item, 162-163
ln (link) command, 33-34, 242
local, 216
logging off, 17
logging on, 13
logging on to another system,
    137-138
login names, 12-13, 216
logout, 216
low-level language, 216
lp (lineprinter) command, 73-77,
    242
lpstat (lineprinter status) command,
    77, 243
ls (list) command, 25-26, 244
ls -l (list -long) command, 25-26,
    36-37

M

-m printing option, 75
-me, 217
-mm, 218
-ms, 218
macro, 217
magnetic tape, 217
mail (mail file) shell variable, 63
mail command, 48-49, 130-132,
    245-247
    options, 131-132
mailx command, 132-135, 247-249
    ? commands, 135
    escape commands, 133-134
    options, 133-135
mainframe, 217
man, 217
mark lists, 161-162
mass storage device, 217
me formatting macro, 154-155
medium, 217
memory, 217
mesg (message) command, 129, 249
messages
    refusing, 129
    sending, 128-129
metacharacters, 85-86, 218
    $, 85-86
    *, 85-86
    ., 85-86
    [ ], 85-86
    \, 85-86
    ^, 85-86
microcomputer, 218
microprocessor, 218
Microsoft XENIX, 9-10
minicomputers, 6-7, 218
mkdir (make directory) command,
    27-28, 249
mm formatting macro, 154-167, 250
    .AL, 163-165
    .B, 167-168
    .BL, 160-162
.DE, 157
.DF, 157
.DL, 161-162
.DS, 157-159
.DS1, 157-159
.DS1Fn, 158-159
.DSC, 159-160
.DSCB, 159-160
.I, 167-168
.ML, 161-162
.P0, 156
.P1, 156-157
.R, 167-168
.RL, 162
.SA, 166
.SPn, 166-167
.Spv, 168-169
.VL, 162-163
modem, 218
more command, 73
motd (message of the day) file, 177
mount, 218
moving files, 30-32
moving text, 116-118
ms formatting macro, 154-155
multi-user systems, system
    administration, 5
Multics, 218
multiplex, 219
multitasking, 3, 53, 219
multiuser, 219
mv (move) command, 30-32, 251

N

neqn, 219
network, 219
newsgroups, 145-150
notations
    binary, 198-199
    octal, 198-199
nroff (new runoff) program,
    154-155, 219, 251-252
numbering systems

283

binary, 198-199
octal, 198-199
numeric conversions, 198-199
numeric notation, 197-198

O

octal (base 8) numbering, 198-199,
219
Open Software Foundation (OSF),
11
opening new lines of text, 110-111
operating systems, 219
DOS, 3
software development, 2
software usage, 2-3
options, 219
-n (numeric), 88-90
-r (reverse), 88-90
printing, 75
sort command, 88-90
ordinary files, 24, 219
OSF *see* Open Software
Foundation
other UNIX systems
communications, 137-138
logging on, 137-138
output, 219
redirecting, 47-51
owner, 219

P

parent directory, 220
passwd (password) command, 15,
252
password file, 220
passwords, 12-13, 220
changing, 15
path (command search path) shell
variable, 63
pathname, 220
PC-based system configuration, 6, 8
peripheral device, 220

permissions, 36-40, 197-199
changing, 38-40, 197
execute, 37-40
numeric notation, 197-198
read, 37-40
symbolic notation, 197
write, 37-40
personal computer, 220
pg (page) command, 72, 253
phototypesetter, 220
pica, 221
pid, 221
pipe, 221
pipeline, 221
pipes, 51-53
point, 221
point size, 168-169
port, 221
portable, 222
Portable Operating System
Environment standard *see* Posix
positional parameters, 58-59
Posix (Portable operating system
environment standard), 11
preprocessor, 222
printing
print queue, 74-77
selecting printer, 76-77
text, 73-77
printing options, 75
-c (copy), 75
-m (mail), 75
processes, 222
accounting, 200
background, 53-55
checking, 55
requesting, 54-55
terminating, 55-56
compared to commands, 47
connecting, 51-53
daemon, 211
foreground, 53
identification number, 222

programming language, 223
programming tools, 5
programs
    nroff (new runoff), 154-155
    roff (runoff), 154-155
    troff (typesetter runoff), 154-155
prompts, 223
    #, 13
    $, 13
    %, 13
ps (process status) command, 55,
    253-254
pwd (print working directory)
    command, 27, 223, 254

Q–R

queue, 223
quizzes, 19-20, 40-42, 66-68, 93-94,
    124-125, 151-152, 170-172,
    202-203
quoting, 223
raw mode, 223
readnews command, 254-255
real-time processing, 223
record, 224
redirecting, 224
    input, 47-51
    output, 47-51
reference lists, 162
refusing messages, 129
regular expressions, 85-86, 224
relative pathname, 224
renaming files, 30
request, 224
restor command, 188
restore, 224
rm (remove) command, 32-33, 255
rmdir (remove directory) command,
    28, 255-256
roff (runoff) program, 154-155
roman text, 167-168, 255
root, 225
root directory, 22-23
RS-232C, 225

S

scrolling, 225
search criteria, 79-81
search path, 225
searching for text, 82-86
security, 36-40, 225
    uucp networks, 143-144
selecting printers, 76-77
self-running processes, 194-195
    daemon processes, 195
sending files, electronic mail,
    138-139
sending messages, 128-129
session, 225
setenv (set environment) command,
    64
sh (shell) command, 256-257
sharing files, 33-34
shell programs, 56
shell prompt, 13, 44-45
shell variables, 63-64
    home (home directory), 63
    mail (mail file), 63
    path (command search path), 63
    term (terminal type), 63
shells, 225
    % prompt, 44
    Bourne shell, 43-44
    C shell, 44
    Korn shell, 44
    shell scripts, 56-62
        interactive, 59-61
    shell variables, 63-64
        home (home directory), 63
        mail (mail file), 63
        path (command search path),
            63
        term (terminal type), 63
Shift-3 (erase character) key, 16
shutdown script, 199-200
shutting system down, 199-200
skipping lines, 166-167
sleep, 226
software, 226

285

development, 2
usage, 2-3
sort command, 86-90, 258
options, 88-90
sorting, 226
fields, 87-88
text, 86-90
special character, 226
special file, 226
special files, 24
stand-alone workstations
configuration, 6-8
standard input, 226
standards, 8
AT&T UNIX, 9-10
Berkeley UNIX BSD, 9-10
CAE, 11
Microsoft XENIX, 9-10
Open Software Foundation, 11
Posix, 11
X Windows, 11
string, 226
stty command, 189-194
su (substitute user) command, 175,
226, 258
subdirectory, 226
superuser, 226
symbolic notation, 197
sync command, 200, 227
system administrator, 173-182
/etc directory, 175-176
backing up files, 182-188
communicating with users,
176-177
daemon processes, 195
log in lists, 181-182
logging in, 175
self-running processes, 194-195
setting up terminals, 188-194
shutting down system, 199-200
system timer, 194-196
user accounts, 177-180

system timer, 194-196
system-to-system communications,
136-138

T

tab, 227
tape drive, 227
tar (tape archive) command, 188,
227
tbl, 227
tee command, 52-53, 139-140, 227,
259
TeleType, 227
term (terminal type) shell variable,
63
termcap (terminal capability) file,
191-194, 227
terminal, 228
terminal-to-terminal
communications, 128-129
terminals
basic settings, 189-194
setting up, 188-194
setup, 12
termcap file, 191-194
terminfo file, 191-194
terminals and minicomputer
configuration, 6
terminfo (terminal information)
file, 191-194, 228
text, 228
bold, 167-168
changing point size, 168-169
entering, 72
formatting, 153-167
display, 157-159
lists, 160-165
paragraphs, 156-157
formatting macros
me, 154-155
mm, 154-167
ms, 154-155

formatting programs
  nroff (new runoff), 154-155
  roff (runoff), 154-155
  troff (typesetter runoff),
    154-155
highlighting, 167-168
italic, 167-168
justifying, 166
printing, 73-77
roman, 167-168
searching, 82-86
skipping lines, 166-167
sorting, 86-90
text editor (vi command), 95-121,
  228
  appending text, 109-110
  command mode, 97
  cursor movement, 98-104
  deleting text, 112-116
  finding and replacing text,
    119-121
  inserting text, 108-109
  moving text, 116-118
  opening new lines, 110-111
  paging, 105
  repeating keystrokes, 100-101
  retrieving files, 99
  saving, 97
  scrolling, 105-106
  undoing keystrokes, 100-101
  zeroing screen, 106-107
text entry mode, 228
text formatter, 228
time-sharing, 228
tmp directory, 22-23
troff (typesetter runoff) program,
  154-155, 228
Trojan horse, 229
tty, 229
typeface, 229
typesetter, 229

U

/usr/spool/uucppublic directory,
  143-144
UNIX
  compared to DOS, 3-5
  shell prompt, 13
  system, 229
  versions, 9-11
UNIX commands table, 4
UNIX-to-UNIX communications,
  140-144
Usenet, 145-150, 230
  newsgroups, 145-150
  reading bulletin board, 147-148
  subscription lists, 149-150
  writing to bulletin board,
    148-149
user accounts, establishing,
  177-180
usr directory, 22-23
uucp (UNIX-to-UNIX copy)
  command, 136-144, 230
uucp networks, 140
  addresses, 142-144
  electronic mail, 141-144
  security, 143-144
uuname command, 137-138
uux command, 144-145

V

variable, 230
variable item lists, 162-163
versions, 9-11
vi (visual interpreter) command,
  95-124, 230
  / (search), 119-120
  a (append), 109-110
  d) (delete sentence), 114-115
  dd (delete line), 113-114
  dw (delete word), 112-113

287

d} (delete paragraph), 115-116
i (insert), 108-109
o (open new line), 110-111
p (put), 117-118
s (substitute), 120-121
subcommand tables, 122-124
x (delete character, 112
volcopy command, 188

W–Z

wall (write-all) command, 176-177
who command, 14, 181-182
wildcard characters, 34-36, 230
   *, 34-36, 85-86
   ?, 34-36
   [x], 34-36
window, 230
word processor, 230
working directory, 230
working environment, 62-64
workstations, 7, 230
   local area network configuration,
   6-7
write command, 128-129
X Windows, 11
XENIX, 231
[ ] metacharacter, 85-86
[x] wildcard character, 34-36
\ metacharacter, 85-86
^ metacharacter, 85-86

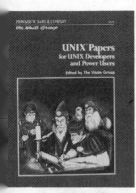

UNIX® Papers
The Waite Group

IX Papers is a collection of select
bers written by well-known UNIX
perts on a broad range of the more
anced cutting-edge topics including
urity, communications, and standards
the operating system. It reveals many
le-known tips and techniques.

4 Pages, 7 1/2 x 9 3/4, Softbound
3N: 0-672-22578-6, $26.95

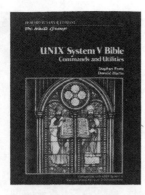

UNIX® System V Bible
Prata and Martin, The Waite Group

This is a comprehensive reference to
UNIX commands and utilities, focusing
on the basic and advanced command
groups found in standard UNIX System V
manuals. Commands are listed
alphabetically and explained in down-to-
earth language. Each entry states the
purpose of a command, what it does, and
how it is used. A graduated set of
example programs goes far beyond the
UNIX Manuals.

528 Pages, 7 1/2 x 9 3/4, Softbound
ISBN: 0-672-22562-X, $24.95

Advanced UNIX® —
A Programmer's Guide
Stephen Prata, The Waite Group

This advanced guidebook goes beyond
the basics of UNIX and spells out the
details of the system's key components
and various programming mechanisms. It
shows how to use simple and complex
commands, including the Bourne Shell,
shell scripts, loops, and system calls; how
to create UNIX graphics; how to allocate
and structure data in memory; and how
to maximize the C-UNIX interface.

496 Pages, 7 1/2 x 9 3/4, Softbound
ISBN: 0-672-22403-8, $24.95

UNIX® Shell Programming for Business
Ray Swartz

Designed for the programmer working in
a business environment, this title shows
how UNIX tools can be used to create a
variety of practical applications designed
specifically for business use. The author
begins with the relatively simple example
of creating and maintaining a list of
seminar attendees. He then explores
creations of greater complexity, including
a general-ledger accounting program, a
time and billing package, a calendar, an
inventory and order entry program, and
more. Each of these examples can be
customized to fit individual needs. The
Bourne shell is discussed with emphasis
on its use in creating business
applications.

400 Pages, 7 3/8 x 9 1/4, Softbound
ISBN: 0-672-22715-0, $26.95

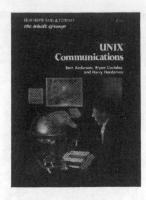

HOWARD W. SAMS & COM.

UNIX® Communications

Anderson, Costales, and Henderson, The Waite Group

Novice or expert UNIX users or programmers will welcome the detailed coverage of UNIX mail, networking, and file transfer tools. The authors show step by step how to use, control, and program UNIX communications tools, give examples of their use, and show how they all fit together.

576 Pages, 7 1/2 x 9 3/4, Softbound
ISBN: 0-672-22511-5, $26.95

Tricks of the UNIX® Masters

Russell G. Sage, The Waite Group

Many of UNIX's most interesting features and capabilities have virtually been kept secret from users.

This book contains the shortcuts, tips, tricks, and secrets programmers need to master UNIX. Text examples are based on an assortment of programming problems ranging from I/O functions and file operations to those involved in porting UNIX to a different computer.

416 Pages, 7 1/2 x 9 3/4, Softbound
ISBN: 0-672-22449-6, $24.95

UNIX® System V Primer, Revised Edition

Waite, Martin, and Prata, The Waite Group

This primer provides a comprehensive overview and introduction to the UNIX System V operating system for the beginning UNIX user. It gives the reader review questions and exercises at the terminal, for an applied, hands-on approach to learning not found in other books on the subject.

456 Pages, 7 1/2 x 9 3/4, Softbound
ISBN: 0-672-22570-0, $22.95

C: Step-by-Step

Mitchell Waite and Stephen Prata, The Waite Group

The first title in the Howard W. Sams Computer Science Series, this entry-level text follows an orderly, methodical fashion to teach the basics of C programming. Designed specifically for one-or-two semester course in C programming, with exercises and quiz throughout.

The book moves through the fundamentals of the C language using practical, logical, interactive tutorials, emphasizing today's methods of structured code, step-wise refinement, and top-down design. An instructor's guide is also available from the author.

600 Pages, 7 1/2 x 9 3/4, Softbound
ISBN: 0-672-22651-0, $27.95

Visit your local book retailer or call
800-257-5755

C Programmer's Guide to Serial Communications
Joe Campbell

book offers a comprehensive
ination of asynchronous serial
nunications. It contains both a
etical discussion of communications
epts and a practical approach to
am design for the IBM PC
onment.

author introduces readers to the
ual" UART, which he uses to
lop a highly portable C programming
y that outperforms costly
nercial products.

Pages, 7 1/2 x 9 3/4, Softbound
: 0-672-22584-0, $26.95

The Waite Group's New C Primer Plus
Mitchell Waite and Stephen Prata

A thorough revision of one of our best-
selling C titles, this user-friendly guide to
C programming is an excellent tutorial
for first-time students of C and a good
reference for experienced C
programmers. It is compatible with UNIX
System V, Microsoft C, Quick C, and
Turbo C.

The book moves through the
fundamentals of the C language using
practical, logical, interactive tutorials. It is
based on the new ANSI C standard, and
all programs include ANSI prototypes.
Today's methods of structured code, step-
wise refinement, and top-down design
are emphasized.

638 Pages, 7 3/8 x 9 1/4, Softbound
ISBN: 0-672-22687-1, $26.95

The Waite Group's Essential Guide to ANSI C
Naba Barkakati

An intermediate-level pocket guide for
programmers, this book conforms to the
American National Standards Institute's
(ANSI) C draft and is the first book on
the newly adopted standard for C. It
provides a convenient and fast reference
to all C functions, with examples for
each, in a handy "shirt-pocket" size.

The book concentrates on the 146
functions in the ANSI C library and
contains debugged real-world examples
for every routine. Each function page
includes a brief tutorial and states the
purpose, syntax, example call, includes,
returns, and "see also" references in
alphabetical format.

224 Pages, 4 1/4 x 8 1/2, Softbound
ISBN: 0-672-22673-1, $7.95

The Waite Group's Essential Guide to Microsoft® C
Naba Barkakati

This conveniently sized reference
organizes and simplifies all 370 functions
in the popular Microsoft C library. In a
user-friendly format, it shows the many
"hidden" routines available to
programmers, providing instant access to
the power of the Microsoft C 5.1
compiler.

304 Pages, 4 3/4 x 8 1/2, Softbound
ISBN: 0-672-22674-X, $7.95

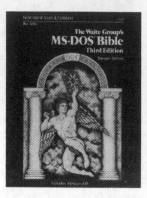

Reader Feedback Card

Thank you for purchasing this book from SAMS FIRST BOOK series. Our intent with this series is to bring you timely, authoritative information that you can reference quickly and easily. You can help us by taking a minute to complete and return this card. We appreciate your comments and will use the information to better serve your needs.

1. Where did you purchase this book?

☐ Chain bookstore (Walden, B. Dalton)   ☐ Direct mail
☐ Independent bookstore   ☐ Book club
☐ Computer/Software store   ☐ School bookstore
☐ Other _____

2. Why did you choose this book? (Check as many as apply.)

☐ Price   ☐ Appearance of book
☐ Author's reputation   ☐ SAMS' reputation
☐ Quick and easy treatment of subject   ☐ Only book available on subject

3. How do you use this book? (Check as many as apply.)

☐ As a supplement to the product manual   ☐ As a reference
☐ In place of the product manual   ☐ At home
☐ For self-instruction   ☐ At work

4. Please rate this book in the categories below. G = Good; N = Needs improvement; U = Category is unimportant.

☐ Price   ☐ Appearance
☐ Amount of information   ☐ Accuracy
☐ Examples   ☐ Quick Steps
☐ Inside cover reference   ☐ Second color
☐ Table of contents   ☐ Index
☐ Tips and cautions   ☐ Illustrations
☐ Length of book
☐ How can we improve this book?_____
☐ _____

5. How many computer books do you normally buy in a year?

☐ 1–5   ☐ 5–10   ☐ More than 10
☐ I rarely purchase more than one book on a subject.
☐ I may purchase a beginning and an advanced book on the same subject.
☐ I may purchase several books on particular subjects.
☐ (such as _____)

6. Have your purchased other SAMS or Hayden books in the past year? _____
If yes, how many _____

7. Would you purchase another book in the FIRST BOOK series? _____

8. What are your primary areas of interest in business software? _____

☐ Word processing (particularly _____)
☐ Spreadsheet (particularly _____)
☐ Database (particularly _____)
☐ Graphics (particularly _____)
☐ Personal finance/accounting (particularly _____)
☐ Other (please specify _____)

Other comments on this book or the SAMS' book line: _____
_____

Name _____
Company_____
Address _____
City _____ State _____ Zip_____
Daytime telephone number _____
Title of this book _____

Fold here

- -